Street by Street

C000216005

NORTHAMI
WELLINGBOROUGH
DAVENTRY, HIGHAM FERRERS,
IRTHLINGBOROUGH, RAUNDS, RUSHDEN
Althorp Park, Blisworth, Bozeat, Brixworth, Bugbrooke, Earls Barton, Finedon, Flore, Irchester, Moulton, Pitsford, Roade, Stanwick, Sywell, Weedon, Wollaston, Wootton

3rd edition June 2008
© Automobile Association Developments Limited 2008

Original edition printed July 2003

 This product includes map data licensed from Ordnance Survey® with the permission of the Controller of Her Majesty's Stationery Office. © Crown copyright 2008. All rights reserved. Licence number 100021153.

Published by AA Publishing (a trading name of Automobile Association Developments Limited, whose registered office is Fanum House, Basing View, Basingstoke, Hampshire RG21 4EA. Registered number 1878835).

Produced by the Mapping Services Department of The Automobile Association. (A03699)

A CIP Catalogue record for this book is available from the British Library.

Printed by Oriental Press in Dubai

Ref: ML144y

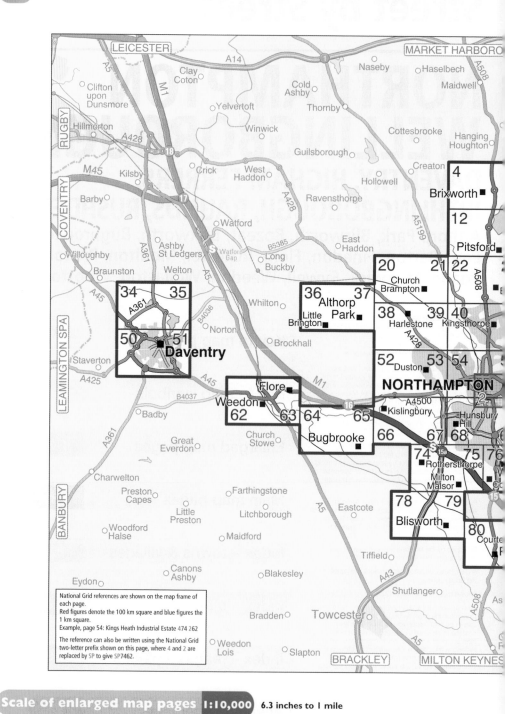

LEICESTER

MARKET HARBORO

A14

Naseby

Haselbech

Maidwell

Clay
Coton

A5

Cold
Ashby

Clifton
upon
Dunsmore

M1

Yelvertoft

Thornby

Cottesbrooke

Hanging
Houghton

RUGBY

Hillmorton

A428

Winwick

Guilsborough

Creaton

M45

Kilsby

Crick

West
Haddon

Hollowell

4

Brixworth ■

Barby

COVENTRY

A428

Ravensthorpe

12

A5199

17

Watford

East
Haddon

Pitsford ■

Willoughby

Ashby
St Ledgers

B5385

Watford
Gap

Long
Buckby

20

21 22

A508

Braunston

A361

Welton

A5

Church
Brampton ■

Whilton

36 37

Althorp
Park ■

38

39 40

A45

34 35

A361

B4038

Little
Brington ■

Harlestone ■

Kingsthorpe ■

Norton

LEAMINGTON SPA

50 51

Daventry ■

Brockhall

A428

52

Duston ■

53 54

Staverton

A45

M1

NORTHAMPTON

A425

B4037

Flore ■

A4500

Kislingbury ■

Hunsbury
Hill ■

Badby

Weedon ■

62

63 64

16

65

Great
Everdon

Church
Stowe

Bugbrooke ■

66

67 68

Charwelton

A5

74 ■
Rothersthorpe

15a

75 76

Preston
Capes

Farthingstone

Eastcote

Milton
Malsor ■

15

Little
Preston

Litchborough

78 79

Woodford
Halse

Maidford

Blisworth ■

80

BANBURY

A361

Tiffield

Courte

Eydon

Canons
Ashby

Blakesley

A43

Shutlanger

A508

Bradden

Towcester

As

National Grid references are shown on the map frame of
each page.
Red figures denote the 100 km square and blue figures the
1 km square.
Example, page 54: Kings Heath Industrial Estate 474 262

The reference can also be written using the National Grid
two-letter prefix shown on this page, where 4 and 2 are
replaced by SP to give SP7462.

Weedon
Lois

Slapton

A5

BRACKLEY

MILTON KEYNES

Scale of enlarged map pages **1:10,000** 6.3 inches to 1 mile

| 0 | 1/4 | miles | 1/2 |
| 0 | 1/4 | 1/2 | kilometres | 3/4 | 1 |

Thorpe
Malsor
CORBY Kettering
A6003
OUNDLE
SP|TL
HUNTINGDON
Cranford
St John
Woodford
Barton
Seagrave
A14
wsley
Broughton
A14
Ringstead
A45
B663
Walgrave
A43
A509
Burton
Latimer
Isham
A510
A6
Great
Addington
Little
Addington
Little
Harrowden
6
7 Finedon
Raunds
10 11
Great
Harrowden
Irthlingborough
8
9
Stanwick
Hargrave
B645
Icot
14 15 16 17 18 19
A509
B571
B645
Chelveston
WELLINGBOROUGH
Higham
Ferrers
Yielden
5 26 27 28 29 30 31-32 33
Sywell
Wilby
Little
Irchester
Rushden
Newton
Bromswold
Knotting
Riseley
Irchester
Wymington
A6
3 44 45 46 47
A4500
Ecton
Earls
Barton
A45
48 49
Wollaston
Hinwick
Souldrop
Sharnbrook
7 58 59
Cogenhoe
1 72 73
Grendon
60 61
Bozeat
Castle
Ashby
Denton
ghton
Felmersham
Bletsoe
Yardley
Hastings
A428
A509
Harrold
Odell
Milton
Ernest
Hackleton
Carlton
Pavenham
Horton
gton
Warrington
B5388
Lavendon
Cold
Brayfield
B565
West End
A428
Oakley
Stevington
Clapham
A6
Olney
Newton
Blossomville
A422
Bromham
Ravenstone
Weston
Underwood
Emberton
Stagsden
Bedford
B526
A509
Astwood
A422
B560
Kempston
B531
MILTON KEYNES
MILTON KEYNES
SP|TL

4.2 inches to 1 mile **Scale of main map pages** 1:15,000

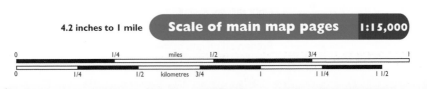

0   1/4   miles   1/2   3/4   1
0   1/4   1/2   kilometres 3/4   1   1 1/4   1 1/2

Junction 9	Motorway & junction
Services	Motorway service area
	Primary road single/dual carriageway
Services	Primary road service area
	A road single/dual carriageway
	B road single/dual carriageway
	Other road single/dual carriageway
	Minor/private road, access may be restricted
← ←	One-way street
	Pedestrian area
	Track or footpath
	Road under construction
	Road tunnel
P	Parking
P+🚌	Park & Ride
🚌	Bus/coach station
	Railway & main railway station
	Railway & minor railway station
⊖	Underground station
⊖	Light railway & station
+++++++++	Preserved private railway

LC	Level crossing
●—●—●—●	Tramway
- - - - - - - -	Ferry route
....	Airport runway
— · — · — · —	County, administrative boundary
▼▼▼▼▼▼▼▼▼▼	Mounds
17	Page continuation 1:15,000
3	Page continuation to enlarged scale 1:10,000
	River/canal, lake, pier
	Aqueduct, lock, weir
465 ▲ Winter Hill	Peak (with height in metres)
	Beach
	Woodland
	Park
	Cemetery
	Built-up area
	Industrial/business building
	Leisure building
	Retail building
	Other building

⊓⊔⊓⊔⊓⊔⊓⊔	City wall		♟	Castle
A&E	Hospital with 24-hour A&E department		⊞	Historic house or building
PO	Post Office		Wakehurst Place (NT)	National Trust property
📖	Public library		Ⓜ	Museum or art gallery
ℹ	Tourist Information Centre		♞	Roman antiquity
ℹ	Seasonal Tourist Information Centre		⚱	Ancient site, battlefield or monument
⛽ ⛽	Petrol station, 24 hour Major suppliers only		⛏	Industrial interest
✝	Church/chapel		✺	Garden
🚻	Public toilets		◉	Garden Centre Garden Centre Association Member
♿	Toilet with disabled facilities		🌱	Garden Centre Wyevale Garden Centre
PH	Public house AA recommended		🌲	Arboretum
⊕	Restaurant AA inspected		🛒	Farm or animal centre
Madeira Hotel	Hotel AA inspected		🦌	Zoological or wildlife collection
🎭	Theatre or performing arts centre		🦅	Bird collection
🎥	Cinema		🦆	Nature reserve
⚑	Golf course		🐟	Aquarium
▲	Camping AA inspected		V	Visitor or heritage centre
🚐	Caravan site AA inspected		⚐	Country park
▲🚐	Camping & caravan site AA inspected		⌒	Cave
⌘	Theme park		✹	Windmill
⌂	Abbey, cathedral or priory		🛢	Distillery, brewery or vineyard

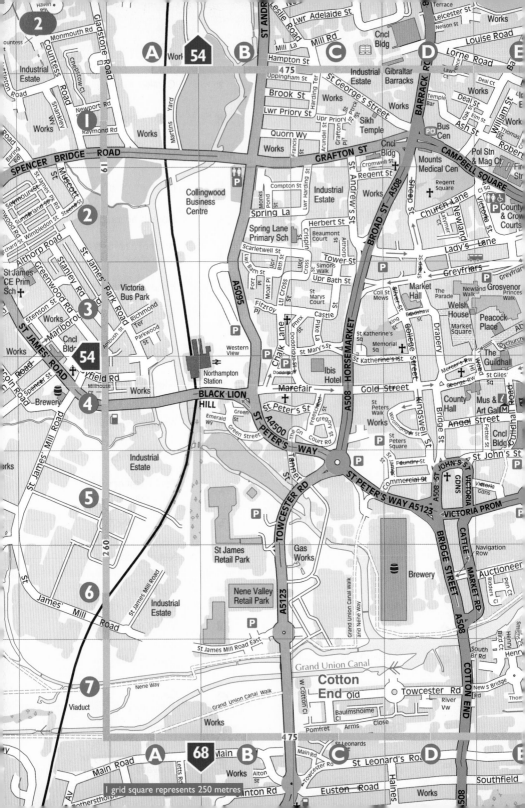

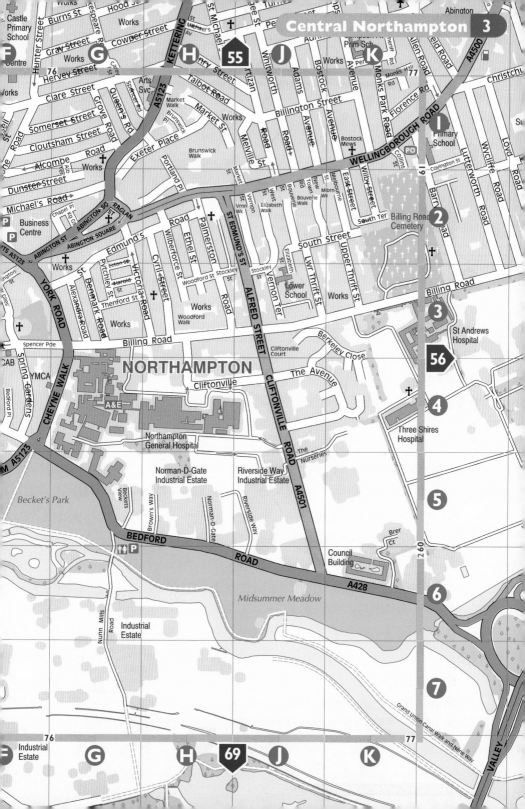

E F G H

Lodge Farm

76

High Street

West End

School Lane

East End

Holcot Lane

Peters Lane

Back Lane

77

I

Scaldwell

72

Scaldwell Road

Rectory Farm

2

Ilmor Avenue

3

Morgan Dr

Scaldwell Road

71

Quarry Rd

Laundon's Lodge

4

Holcot Road

Holcot Road

Burrows Vale

Way

The Ridings

Grass State Conswll

The Ashway

The Knoll

A508

The Ashway

5

Grange Farm

270

E F G H

76 77

13

6

Frisby Lodge

A

Finedon Sta.

B

Hillsboro Farm

C

D

Furnace Lane

4 88

89

A509

River Ise

1

Furnace Lane

Furnace Cottages

TOP ROAD B574

Hill Top Road

Hill Top

KETTERING ROAD

2

Shortlands Lodge

3

Golf Course

Great Harrowden Lodge

B574

INGBURY ROAD

71

Wellingborough Golf Club

The Slips

ork Lane

Manor Close

4

The Slips

Wentworth Farm

Great Harrowden

Finedon Road Industrial Estate

Grammarians FC

Bradfield Close

Bradfield Road

Vaux Road

Yelden Cl

Sanders Road

Wellingborough Road

A509

5

Grange Road

Holme Cl

The Meadows

The Fairway

The Downs

Giltrey Cl

Appleby Cl

The Glade

Way

The Partures

The Banks

Oak Vw

Bridle Close

Stewarts Road

Sanders Cl

Finedon Road Industrial Estate

Fine Indu

270

4 88

89

A509

Redhill

Fallowfield

A

Fallowfie

15

The Banks

B

NORTHEN WAY

Goodwin Cl

Soane

Crome Cl

Soane Cl

Dhc Vw

An Cl

C

Stanton Cl

16

WARTS ROAD

Sanders

Lloyd

Fulmar

D

Wilkie Road

I grid square represents 500 metres

E F G H

95 96

Freestones
Lodge

Knightlands

I

72

Nene Way

Welford Cl
Rugby Dr
Fird
Gardenfields
Churchill Av
Langley Crs
Fettledine Road
Addington Road
Welford Avenue
Noble Av

The Shortlands
Alexander Rd
Palmer Avenue
Alexander
Place

Clarke
Cl

NN9

2

Crow
Hill

Addington Road

3

River Nene Navigation

By-Pass
Farm

71

A6

Long Acres
Mddl Grss
Wicken Cl
Merefields
Mountfield Rd
Knightlands Rd
Drayton Road
Portland Rd
Scharpwell
Drayton
Fremor Rd
Er Dr
Hough Way
WENEDON ROAD

J Attley Wy
Diamond Way

Rushden &
Diamonds FC
(Nene Park)

Station Road

B571
ADDINGTON RD

STATION ROAD

Works
Lovell
Ct
Highfield Rd
Fernmoor
New St
Lilley Ter
Sg St
Works

Diamond
Way

3

PO
B5348
Scarborough
Street
Nursery Gdns
College Street
Jun Sch
Inf Sch
Manton Rd
Musson Rd
WEBEDON ROAD

H

Lime St
Nene Vw
Church St
Lime
Ter
Mth Sci

STATION ROAD

4

Viaduct

B571
Lees St
St Peter's Wy
Oak
Sy Rd
Civic
Hall
St Peter's Church
Cemetery

Medical Cen
BriarCt

Park Rd
Baker St
Cherry St
John
Pyel
Road
Crouch Rd
Meadow Wy
Allen Rd Nicholas Rd

Nene Way

5

270

Chowns Mill
Business Park

A45

HIGH STREET
Green Cl
Victoria Street
Hayway
Whites Cl
Allen Road
Vale Road
Randall

E F G **19** H

95 96

A6

A45

A5028

CHOWNS MILL
ROUNDABOUT

Ullswater Rd
Windermere Dr
Eskn Cl
A5028 STATION

12

A B **4** C D

473
70

1

69

2

3

268

4

5

473

A B **22** C D

Park Farm

Froxhill Crescent

St Davids Close

Pytchley Court Health Ce

Froxhill Crescent

Dairy Cl

elleycotes Rd

Broad

Windmill

Old

Stonehill Way

Northa

Northampton Road

74

Victors Barns

Merry Tom Lane

74 Pitsford
odge Farm

on Lane

1 grid square represents 500 metres

E F 5 76 G H Grange Farm 77 70

1

Brixworth Country Park

Pitsford Reservoir

2 Moulton Grange Farm

69

Moulton Grange

Grange Lane

3

Works Works Grange Lane

4

Works

NN6

Grange

Springhill Farm The Dovecote Church La Manor Rd Broadlands 268

Pitsford Primary Sch Glebe La Manor Rd The Chase

PO The St High St Drummond Close **Pitsford**

High Street 5

Northamptonshire Grammar School Stable Ct

Home Farm E F 76 **23** G H 77

Stud Farm

Moulton

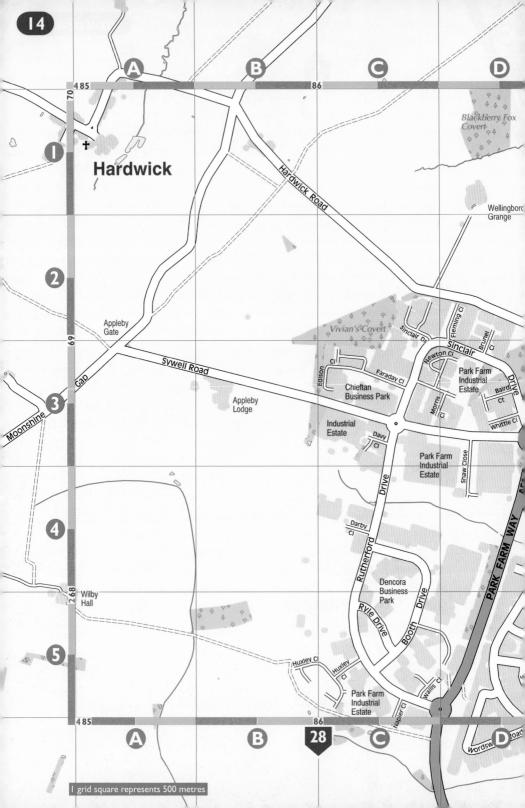

14

485 **70** 86

A **B** **C** **D**

Blackberry Fox
Covert

1 †
Hardwick

Hardwick Road

Wellingborough
Grange

2 69

Appleby
Gate

Vivian's Covert

Sinclair Dr

Fleming Cl

Brunel
Cl

Sinclair

Sywell Road

Edison

Cl

Faraday Cl

Newton Cl

Morris
Cl

Park Farm
Industrial
Estate

Drive

Baird
Ct

Whittle Cl

3 Gap
Moonshine

Appleby
Lodge

Chieftan
Business Park

Industrial
Estate

Davy
Cl

Park Farm
Industrial
Estate

Shaw Close

Darby
Cl

Rutherford

Drive

4

2 68
Wilby
Hall

Dencora
Business
Park

Booth

Drive

Ryle Drive

PARK FARM WAY A509

5

Huxley Cl

Huxley
Cl

Wallis Cl

Napier Cl

Park Farm
Industrial
Estate

485 86

A **B** **28** ▾ **C** **D**

Wordsworth Road

I grid square represents 500 metres

E
7 Carrol Spri Farm F
G
8
H

Sidegate La

West Field Lodge

I

WELLINGB

Finedonhill Farm

Sidegate Lane

Stone Cross Farm

2

MILL ROAD

B571

69

South Hill Farm

IRTHLINGBOROUGH ROAD

South View Farm

3

18

Ditchford Road

Irthlingborough Grange

Works

4

268

5

E
F
31 Nene Way
G
H

18

A 8 B C D

70 493

WELLINGBOROUGH ROAD

B571

West Field
Lodge

† Cemetery

1

Green
Close

Presland

AM

Ebbw Vale Road
94
MC
Diamond Dr

Cherry St
WHITES RY
Allen Road
Hayway
John
Pyel
Road
Allen Rd Nicholas Rd

WELLINGBOROUGH ROAD

Crouch Rd

Wm Trigg Cl
Randall
Cl

Thomas Flawn Road

BL WK
Milton Walk
Gr Wk
The
Sidings

Ringtail Cl

Dairy

Evensford
Wrt

Vale Road

Reservoir Cl

C W Wk

W W Wk

Broadholme

Waterloo Wy
Lkesd

Waterloo Wy

Ebbw
Cl

Rehill
Cl

OsEC

Lodge Wy

Joan Pyel
Cl

Home Cl

Lakeside

2

69

Treatment Works

3

17

Nene Way

River Nene

4

ks

Nen
Val
Farr

B645
Brindley Cl

5

268

Works

Travelodge

A5001
Superstore

Pegasus
Wy

Cole St

Francis Ct

Crown Way

Works

Parkham
Industrial
Estate 94

Norris Wy

Norris

493

A B 32 C D

NORTHAMPTON ROAD A5001

A45

Sanders Lodge
Industrial Estate

Palm Rd

WELLINGBOROUGH

Paddocks Rd

Chestnut
Cl

1 grid square represents 500 metres

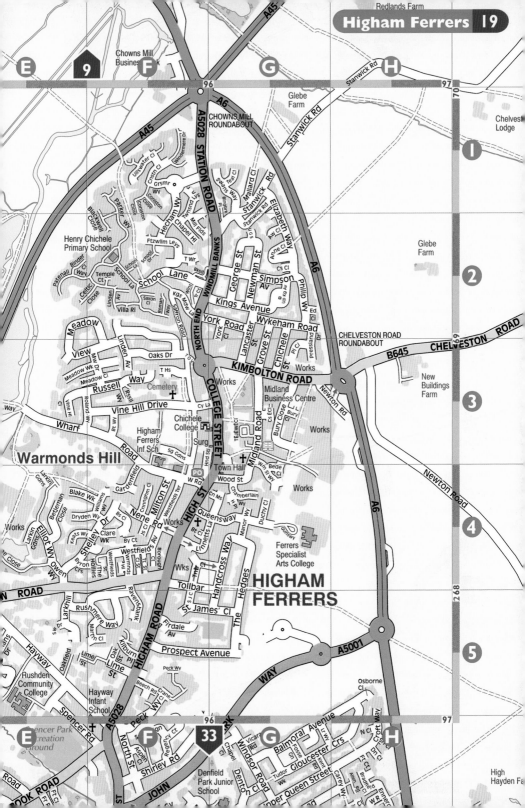

Redlands Farm

Chowns Mill Business Park

E 9 F G Stanwick Rd H

Chelves Lodge

Glebe Farm

CHOWNS MILL ROUNDABOUT

Henry Chichele Primary School

Simpson Av

Kings Avenue

York Road

Wykeham Road

CHELVESTON ROAD ROUNDABOUT

Glebe Farm

CHELVESTON ROAD

B645

Meadow View

Russell Way

Cemetery

Vine Hill Drive

KIMBOLTON ROAD

Midland Business Centre

Works

New Buildings Farm

Wharf

Chichele College

Higham Ferrers Inf Sch

Town Hall

Wood St

Works

Newton Road

Warmonds Hill

PO

Works

Ferrers Specialist Arts College

Queensway

HIGHAM FERRERS

Works

Tollbar

James' Cl

Prospect Avenue

Firdale Av

Rushden Community College

Hayway Infant School

A5001

WAY

Osborne Cl

Spencer Park Recreation Ground

E F 33 G H

Denfield Park Junior School

Upper Queen Street

High Hayden Fa

20

Holdenby
House

Falconry Centre

✠ **A**

Holdenby

B

C

D

4 69

70

1

67

2

Holdenby
South Lodge

3

66

4

37

5

A428

Glebe
Farm

Glebe   Lane

2 65

4 69

70

A

B

38

C

D

Lower
Harleston

1 grid square represents 500 metres

E   F   *Sander's Covert*   72   G   H   73

Merry Tom Lane

I

Spinney Farm

67

WELFORD ROAD

2

Brampton Hill

Midshires Way

A5199

Chapel Brampton

Cedar Hythe

Back Lane

NN6

Great Close

Little Cl

Pitsford Road

3

22

Church Farm

Harlestone Road

The Bramptons Primary School

Spencer Cl

66

Stables La

Manor Farm

Church Lane

Walkers La

NORTHAMPTON ROAD

4

Sandy Lane

Golf Lane

Brampton Grange

Church Brampton

Brampton Heath Golf Centre

Golf Course

Northamptonshire County Golf Club

Golf Course

5

Works

265

72   73

E   F   39   G   *Covert*   H

High St

Stable Ct

Northamptonshire
Grammar School

E   **F**   13   **G**   **H**

76   77

Home
Farm

Moulton Road

Stud
Farm

I

Pitsford Road

Fox Covert
Hall

2

Bunkers
Hill Farm

Butcher's Lane

3

24

Boughton

Butcher's La

Spring Cl

Church St

Boughton
Primary School

Spectacle Lane

Holly
Lodge

4

Humfrey Lane

Moulton Lane

Greville
Cl

Howard Lane

Devonshire
Cl

Boughton
Green

Obelisk

Spinney Cl

Boughton Green Road

Lower Farm Road

Industrial
Estate

5

Ash Rise

Obelisk Rise

Obelisk Rise

Tenter   Road

Duncan
Cl

E   **F**   41   **G**   **H**

76   77

RED HOUSE ROAD

265

St John's Av

Rev

Way

Dixon Rd

Moulton
Business
Park

Magistrates
Court

**Moulton
Park**

Sunnyside
Lower School

All Saints CE VA
Primary School

Holly Ldg
Dr

Kings Park Rd

Summerhouse Road

Deer

N2

24

A B C D

477 Moulton Lodge Boughton Fair Lane 78

Holcot Road

1

Pitsford Road

2 Home Farm

Browns Cl

Church Vw The Grove Grove Farm La

Allbone Cl

Homestead Cl

Stewart Close T Hills The Lrhs Moulton Primary School Py VW

3 Jeyes Cl Moulton College West St Church Hill High St The Crs Prince of Wales RW

23 Boughton Road Carey Cl West Street Church St PO Dove's La Oakley Dr

Enyon Cl Pound Lane Cross St Barlow La

Moulton School Pound Lane Av Gs

Lunchfield La

Moulton Manor Road Surgery

Whiting Ct Brunting Rd Northampton Lane North

4 Holly Fuller Road

New Manor Farm Harvey La Ryland Rd

Greenwood Cl

Hrs Will Ct

Gayhurst Cl Southcroft E Ct West Leys St E Leys Ct Glengary

5 Lower Farm Road Medbourne Cl Cottingham Dr Kings Meadow Sch Rides Ct Lowick Court Thorpeville

Tenter Road Brdn Cl Cedar Gate

RED HOUSE ROAD A5076 265 Northampton Lane South Manning Road WAY

Magistrates Court 477 Boughton 78 Woodru Underbank

Moulton Park **A** Moulton Park Business Cen **B** Lane **42** Crowberry **C** Leaf **D** Sileby Rangers FC

Deer Park Road Pond Wd Dr Industrial Booth Rl

1 grid square represents 500 metres Brickyard Quarry Cubleigh

E   F   G   H

84   85

The Grange

Highfield Road

Glebe Road

I

67

Mears Ashby Endowed Primary School

North Street

Tinkers Crs

Manor Road

Church Street

Bakehouse

Nursery Ct

Wellingborough Road

Mears Ashby

2

Earls Barton Road

Vicarage La

Paddock Cl

Lady's Lane

Wilby Road

Duchess End

Sywell Road

Hill Farm

NN6

3

28

66

4

I Reservoir

Sywell Country Park

P

Washbrook Lane

Mears

5

265

E   F   G   H

84   45   85

Ashby Road

White House Industrial Estate

Main R Farm

MAIN ROAD

28

A   B   14   C   D

485   86

1

67

2

Mears Ashby Road

Wilby

3

27

Willby CE
Primary
School

4

66

5

265

485   86
A   B   46   C   D

White House
Industrial Estate

ROAD

Earls Barton
Cemetery

Wellingboro

Huxley Cl

Huxley
Cl

Park F
Industrial
Estate

Napier Cl

Wallis Cl

BOO

SW

Wordsworth Road

PARK FARM W

Doddington Road

M Road
Farm

1 grid square represents 500 metres

32

A   B   C   D

Brindley Cl

Travelodge

A5001

Superstore

493

Pegasus Wy

Francis Ct

18

Works

Crown Way

P
Indus'9 4il
Estate

NORTHAMPTON ROAD A5001

A45

A5001

Norris Way

Norris Wy

Paddocks Rd

WELLINGBOROUGH

Palm Rd

Fern Rd

ROAD

Chestnut
Cl

Sanders Lodge
Industrial Estate

Shipton Way

Express
Business Park

Masefield Drive

Holly
Rd

Keats Way

Keats Wy

Glenfield Cl

Gravely St

B569

Melloway

Road

Silverdale
GV

Dingle
Road

Purbeck Rd

Farndish
Cl

Cresswell
Rd

Birchal

IRCHESTER ROAD

2

Westfield Avenue

Boundary Av

Tennyson Rd

Highfield Road

Rose

67

Knuston

Home
Farm

PO

Church Hall Rd

Morris Av

Whitefriars

Blackfriars

Farnha

3

31

STATION ROAD

66

ial

ower
arm

4

Knuston
High Farm

ge Rd

Arkwright

Denton
Cl

Manor
Cl

Norman
Wy

Saxon Ri

Austin Cl

Road

Parsons Rd

Warren Cl

Evelyn
Wy

Rmn Wy

Lyneford

Balhai

265

chester

5

493

94

A   B   C   D

Irchester
Grange

Northamptonshire County
Bedfordshire County

Road

1 grid square represents 500 metres

Moor Farm

I

Glebe Farm

A B C D

4 65 66

66

2

Whilton Rd

Back La

Main St

Main Street

✝

Grea Bring

PO PH

65

Back Lane

Hamilton Lane

3

4

Brington Primary School

✝

2 64

5

Folly Lane

PH

Main Street

Blacksmiths Lane

Hall Lane

Pine Ct

Steeple Lane

Little Brington

Church Farm

4 65 66

A B C D

✝

Hillcrest Cottage

I grid square represents 500 metres

Works

E F G H

68 69

66

Macmillan Way

I

20

NN7

2

Sir John's Wood

Althorp

65

Dog
Pond

Althorp
Park

Chinkwell
Spinney

Oaktree
Stew

3

Great
Stew

Garden
Stew

Harleston
Forest

4

264 38

Yew Tree
Farm

Harles

5

68 69

E F G res Way H

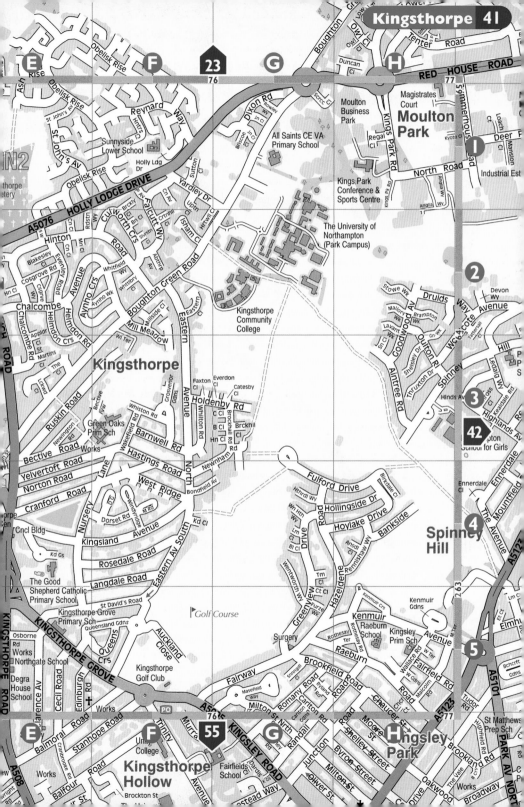

44

Golf Course

Ecton
Belt

Ecton Field
Plantation

26

Ecton
North Lodge

481

82

A

B

C

D

Poundel

Blackthorn
Wood

Woodland Wy

Ecton
West Lodge

The
World's End
Hotel

Viscount Road

Emlington Rd

Prtch

Ft Cl

Pilton

Wellingborough Road

Leyside Ct

Talan Rd

Shire Pl

Jasmine Ln Sq

Mortar Pit Rd

Crowthorp Rd

Felmead Road

Conweston Rd

Rectory
Farm

Erxmine Rd

Lowlands Close

Wright Rd

Niard Close

Rd

Church
VW

Northmoor Rd

Franklin's Cl

Parsons
Cl

Ecton Village
Primary
School

Church
WV

Dore Close

Rectory
Farm
Primary
School

Olden Rd

Riley

Deacons
Ct

Bentley Close

Morgan Cl

Deansway

Daimler Cl

Healey Cl

Botmead Road

Hurstmead

Jerry Ri

Berrydale

E

Blackthorn
Primary
School

Pack Ml Ct

Hpmdw Ct

Great Mdw Rd

Oleander Crs

Thornfeld

Thornapple

Prescott

Custom Rise

West Street

High Street

Church
WV

3

Cherry Ldg Road

Beaumont Drive

Tiptoe

Asp

Santou Avenue

Strawberry Hl

Hdge

The
Laurels

43

thorn

Collings

Cowgill

Coniston Cl

Great Billing Way

WELLINGBOROUGH ROAD

Maidencastle

Maidencastle

Peile Dr

Valentine Wy

Penfold Lane

A5076

Clig Fld

Newstead

Woburn Rd

Lakeside Dr

Sheerwater
Dr

4

Chantry Cl

Penfold
Gardens

Ecton

Park Road

Wimborne

Vantage
Meadow

Great
Billing

Lady Winefrede's

Oransay Cl

Cumbrae Dr

Hall Place

Rsns Flo

Southern

Ecton Brook
Linear Park

Church Walk

Elwes
Way

Pound

High Street

Lismore

Blueberry

Hl Sq

Winstr

Overmead Road

Nrmd Sq

Ecton Brook
Primary
School

Parkside

Ecton Brook Road

Millbank

Ecton
Brook

5

Bellinge

St Andrews
CE Primary
School

Station Rd

Cattle Hl

Shepperton

Ham Meadow

Oat Hill Drive

Sit Sq

Fxndl Sq

Hrsmr

Blirps

PO
Med
Cen

Riverwell

Chedworth

Ecton
Brook

Camberley
Close

Bellinge
Primary
School

Mill Rd

Kiltroft
Court

Lasham Ct

Pennycress Pl

Ecton Brook Road

58

A45

481

82

A

B

C

D

Campion Court

Coneygate Ct

Faracre Ct

Glade Road

1 grid square represents 500 metres

46

A B 28 C D

485
65

Main Road
Farm

White House
Industrial Estate

MAIN ROAD

Earls Barton
Cemetery

The
Grange

Industrial
Estate

Titley Bawk Av

Wellingborough Road

Barton Av

Mallard Close

NORTHAMPTON ROAD

Elizabeth Way

Hornby Rd

The Pightle

North
Road

KING Street

Grange Cl

Streeton Wy

Townley Wy

White Wy

Elizabeth
Cl

Ctr Cl

Victoria St

Manor Road

Prince Street

Whitworth
Crescent

Berry

Queen St

Manor House
Close

High Street

The Dell

Knights Cl

Tebburts Cl

Stevens
Ct

New Barton

Harrowick La

Surg

Churchill Road

Mills Close

Spencer Cl

St Crispin Road

WEST STREET

B573

Earls Barton
Jun Sch

Farhurst

Fair

Clarke
Court

DODDINGTON ROAD

Woodlands
Grange

Glebe
Farm

Park Cl

PO

BROAD STREET

Blackwell
Cl

Works

London
End

45

Aggare Wy

Saxon Cl

Wilson Way

Barker Road

Dowthorpe
End

Sheffield Wy

Spring Gardens

New St

Mt
Pleasant

Shurville
Cl

Dowthorpe

Milbury

HILL

Cowper Cl

Gray Cl

Burns
Cl

Cordon Cs

Keats
Cl

Clare
Cl

Nene Way

Mill
Lane
Farm

4

Shoemakers Cl

Station Road

Allebone
Road

Oxford
Close

Balmoral
Close

Earls Barton

263

Compton Way

Thorpe Rd

A45

5

485
Grendon Road

86

A B C D

Station Road

Way

1 grid square represents 500 metres

Great
Doddington **29**

E   F   G   H

88   **89**   **65**

Wilby Lane

A45

Goodens Lane

Great Doddington
Primary School

Top
Farm
La

Glebe Farm
Court

Church

John Gray Road

Nene Way

PO

HIGH STREET

St Nicholas
Rd

Frost
Court

Lower Street

I

ROAD

EARLS

BARTON

Glenfield Drive

Nene Way

River Nene

2

64

Debdale
Spring Farm

Hardwater

Summer Leys
Nature Reserve

3

Hardwater
Mill

Road

4

P

Ryeholmes
Bridge

Nene Way

Works

263

48

Crin
Cott

5

E   F   G   H

88   **89**

Long
Lodge Farm

The Old
Lodge

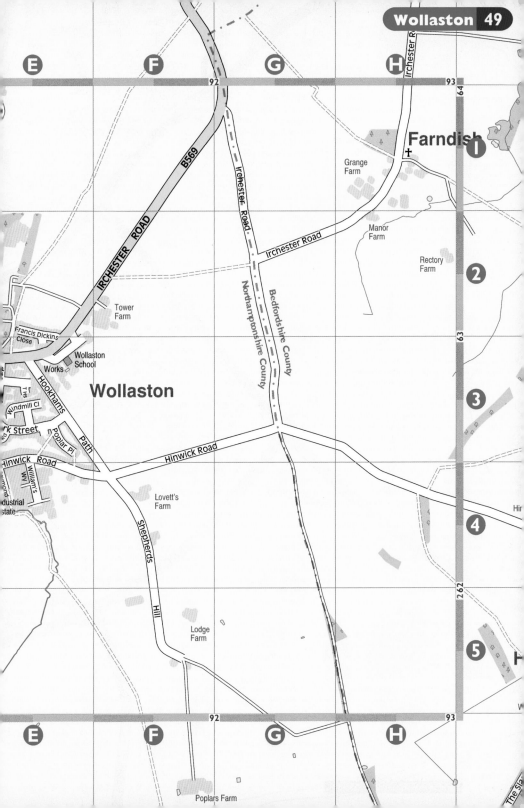

E F G H

92 93

64

Irchester R

Farndish 1

†

Grange
Farm

Manor
Farm

Irchester Road

Rectory
Farm 2

63

Northamptonshire County

Bedfordshire County

Irchester Road

B569

IRCHESTER ROAD

Tower
Farm

Francis Dickins
Close

Wollaston
School

Works

Wollaston

T HS

Windmill Cl

Hookhams
Path

Poplar Pl

k Street

Hinwick Road

Hinwick Road 3

Lovett's
Farm

William's
Wy

ndustrial
state

Shepherds
Hill

Lodge
Farm

Hir

4

262

H 5

E F G H

92 93

W

Poplars Farm

The S12

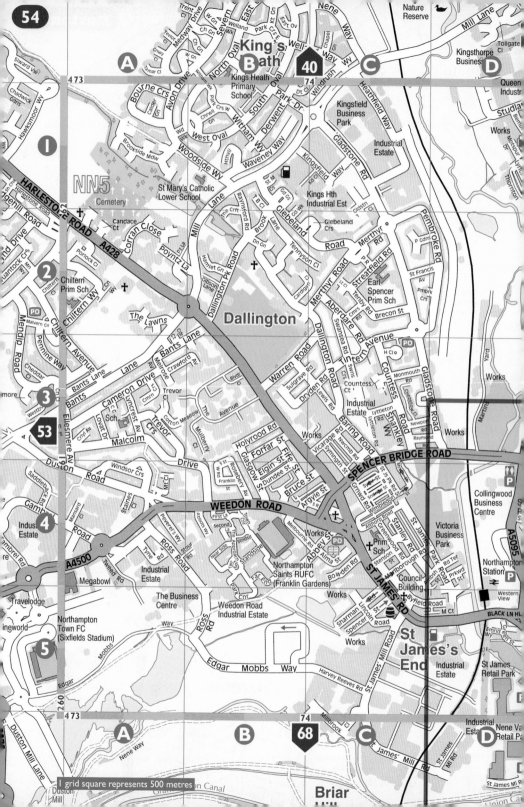

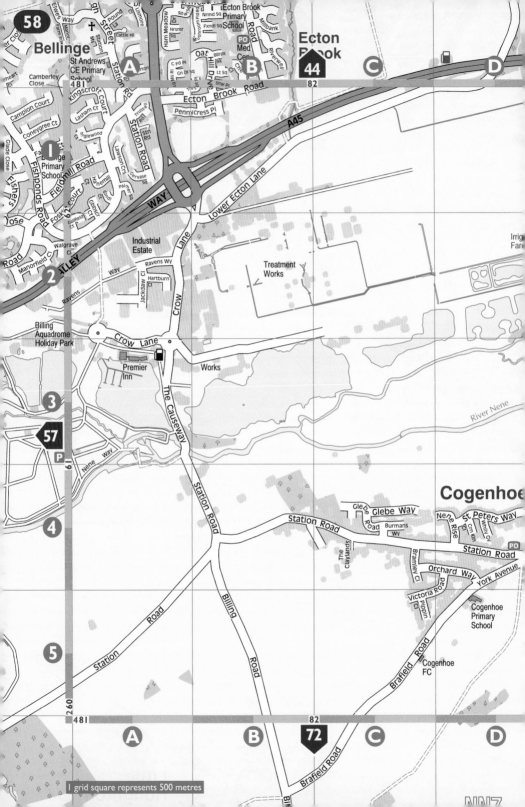

58
Bellinge

Elvers Way
Farm Rd
Manor
High Street
Pound
Cattle Hi
Ham Meadow
Hrsmr
Ecton Brook
Ecton Brook
Primary
School
Minbank
Riverwell

St Andrews
CE Primary
School

A
Station Rd
B
Med
Cen
PO

Ecton Brook

44
82
C
D

Camberley
Close
481
Kingscroft Court

Campion Court

Coneygree Ct

Lasham Ct
Kingscroft Court
Glewood

Oat
Hill Drive
Ecton Brook Road

Pennycress Pl

A45

Fairfield
Primary
School

Fieldmill Road

Fishponds Road

Foskett Court

Fishponds Road

Glade Close

Fisher's Close

Fisher's Close

Road

I

Palmer Sq

Gaitfield

Hartham

Way

Lower Ecton Lane

Walgrave
Ct

Manorfield Ct

2
VALLEY

Ravens

**Industrial
Estate**

Ravens Wy

Jackdaw Cl
Hartburn
Cl

Crow Lane

**Treatment
Works**

Irrig
Farm

Billing
Aquadrome
Holiday Park

Crow Lane

Crow Lane

Works

River Nene

3

Premier
Inn

The Causeway

57
P
6

Nene Way

4

Station Road

Station Road

Glebe
Road
Glebe Way

Burmans
Wy

Cogenhoe

Nene Rise

St Peters Way

Whitly Cl

Crn Kln

PO

The Claylands

Bramley Cl

Station Road

Orchard Way

Pippin Cd

York Avenue

5

Station Road

Billing Road

Victoria Rd

Brafield Road

Cogenhoe
FC

Cogenhoe
Primary
School

260
481

A
B

82

72
C
D

Brafield Road

NN7

I grid square represents 500 metres

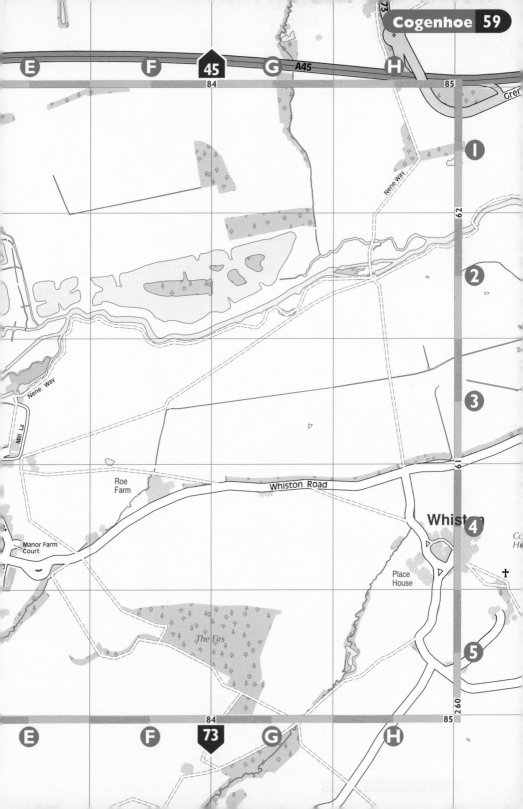

E F **45** G A45 H

84 85

Gren

1

Nene Way

62

2

Nene Way

3

19

Mill La

Roe
Farm

Whiston Road

Whist n

4

Manor Farm
Court

Place
House

Co
H

†

The Firs

5

260

84 85

E F **73** G H

E F G H

90 91

61

Greenfield
Lodge

1

2

60

WOLLASTON ROAD

Red Gables
Farm

3

Wollaston Road

Fullwell Rd

Fullwell Rd

Wollaston Rd

Hope St

Fullwell Rd

Council Street

Bull Cl

Allens

Glebe
Farm

Harrold Road

Harrold Road

Pear Tree Close

Hill

4

Slype
Farm

Hensmans La

Cn Fm Cl

Bozeat
Primary
School

The Orch

Manor Cl

Cemetery

Mile Street

Pudding Bag La

Dychurch Lane

259

Easton Lane

Easton Lane

Road

High St

Church La

Wheelwrights

A509

Mill Rd

Selby Gdns

W H

Wyman Cl

PO

Brookside

5

Stoney Piece Cl

Abbey Cl

Queen St

Mill Road

Clayland Cl

London St

Man

Hewlett's Cl

Road

Hillside

Knights La

Flr Tree Gv

Flr Tree Gv

Bozeat

Roberts Street

Little Cl

E F G H

Low
Farm

90 91

White House
Farm

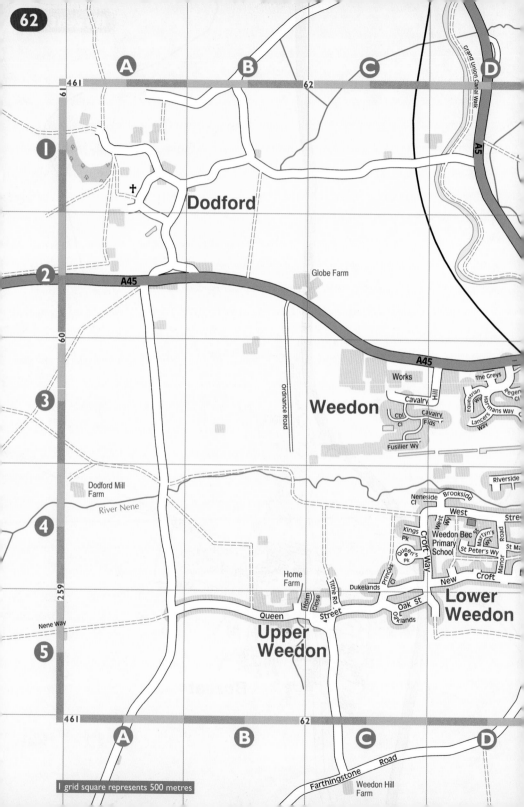

A **B** **C** **D**

461
61
62

1

†

Dodford

Grand Union Canal Walk

A5

2
A45

Globe Farm

60

A45

3

Works

The Greys

Cavalry Hill

Equestrian Wy

Regent Cl

Hartmans Way

Lancers Way

Weedon

Cbl Cl

Cavalry Flds

Fusilier Wy

4

Dodford Mill Farm

River Nene

Ordnance Road

Riverside

Neneside Cl

Brookside

West Wy

West Road

Stre

St Ma

Kings Pk

Weedon Bec Primary School

Martyn's Wy

St Peter's Wy

259

Queen's Pk

Croft Way

Croft

Manor Road

Home Farm

Princes

Dukelands

New

Lower Weedon

Holm Close

Tithe Rd.

Oak St

Oaklands

Queen Street

5

Nene Way

Upper Weedon

461
62

A **B** **C** **D**

Farthingstone Road

Weedon Hill Farm

Oxhouse Farm

E F G H

64 M1 65 61

I

Hillside Road

Mussott Close

Sears Cl

Brockhall Road

The Crs

Collins Hill

Flore Hill Farm

Capell Rise

2

FLORE HILL

Flore Hill

A45

HIGH

PO

Yew Tree

Sutton St

Gdns

Sutton

King's Lane

Bliss La

STREET

Acre

The Grn

The Orch

Sgfd

Spring Lane

Chapel La

Meadow Farm Cl

The Avenue

Brickett's

Thornton Cl

Chapel La

Road Weedon

Flore CE Primary School

The Avenue

Spring La

Chapel La

Flore

60

Flore Park

Nene Way

3

The Mill Farm

Grand Union Canal

4

Church Street

Billing Sch

Pl

Weedon Cemetery

Whitehall Farm

Weedon ec

259 64

Works

5

A5

Macmillan Way

E F G H

64 65

Tanborough

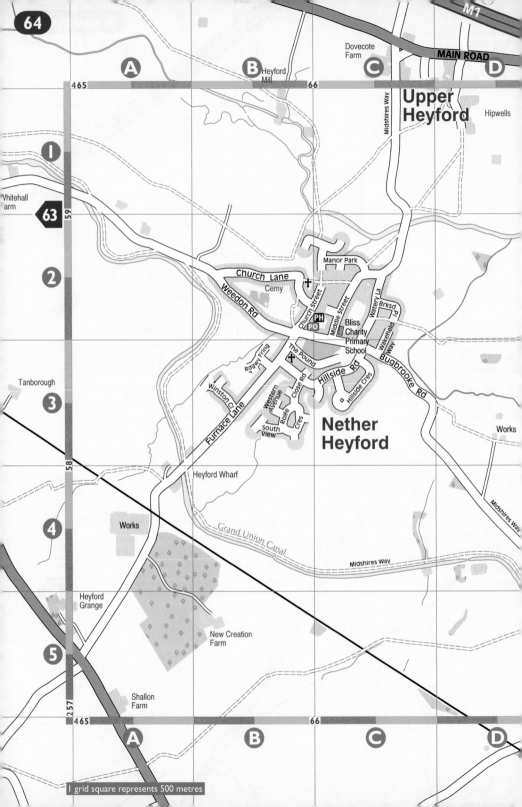

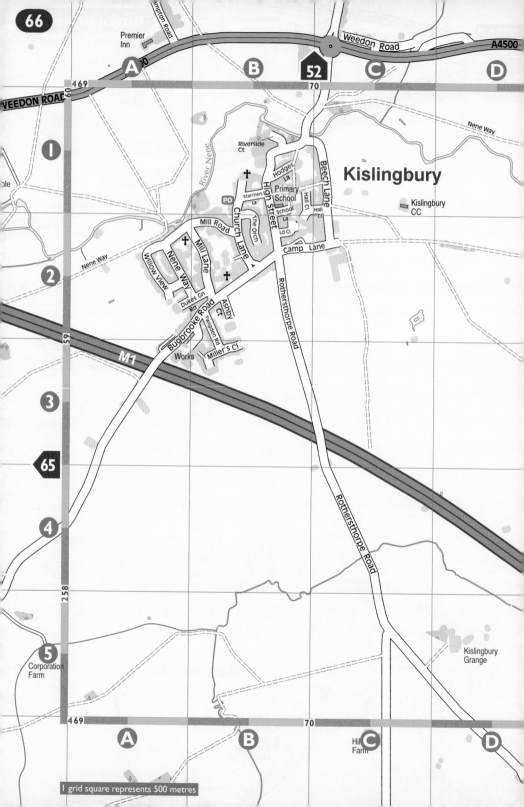

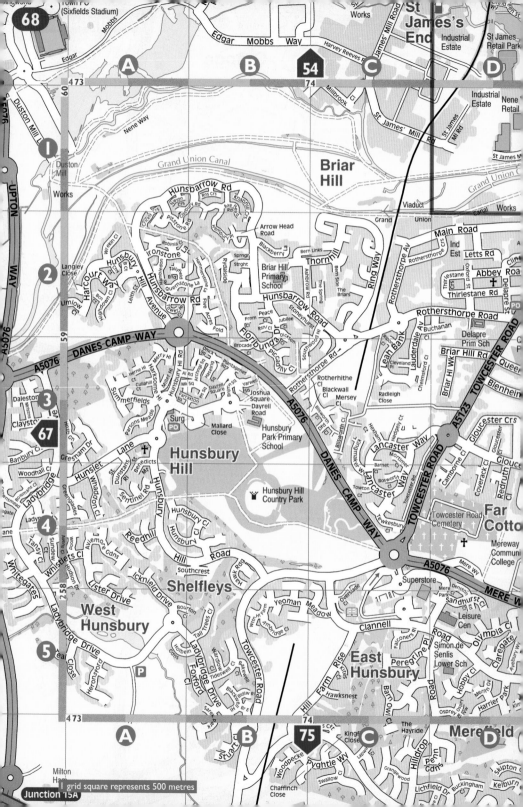

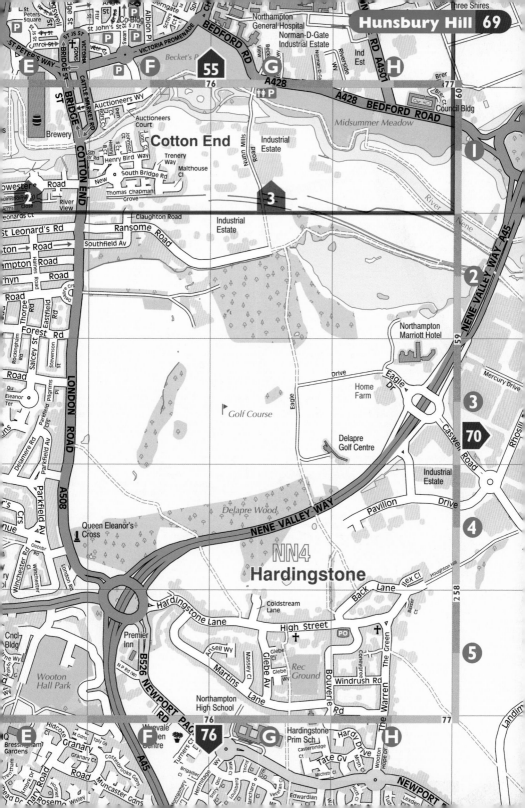

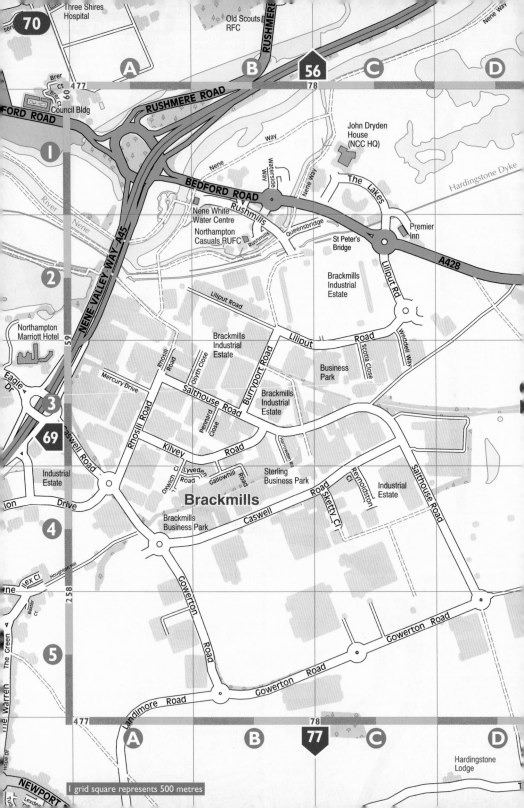

E F 57 G H

80

60

Little Houghton

Grange Farm

Nursery Close

Meadow Lane

Station Road

I

Bedford Road

PO

Lodge Road

Home Acre

Bedford Road

Little Houghton CE Primary School

Lodge Cl

81

Bedford Road

Great Houghton Cemetery

A428

2

59

Cherry Tree La

The Cross

igh Street

Willow Lane

Little La

The Hill

Glebe La

Chestnuts La

Willow Crescent

Dobson Close

Atterbury Wy

Lodge Road

3

72

Paget Close

Wynersley Cl

Farm Wy

Lime

The Green

Keats Cl

Little Houghton Lodge

4

258

Leys Lane

5

80

81

E F G H

Great Houghton Lodge Farm

72

A B 58 C D

481 82

60

1

Station

Road

Brafield Road

Cogenhoe FC

Billing Road

Brafield Road

NN7

2

Bedford Road

Lower End

St. Thomas Rd

Cares Orchard

Long Acre

Grove Rd

✝

59

Bedford Rd

Home Farm

3

71

Bridle Cl

BEDFORD

Chapel Lane

✝ PO

ROAD

Church La

Brafield-on-the-Green

Elm Close

Mere Cl

Green Rd

Park Cl

Furze Rd

4

Horton Road

258

5

481 82

A B C D

Horton Road

Mere Barn

I grid square represents 500 metres

E   F   59   G   H

84   85

I

2

3

Chadstor

4

5

The Firs

Whiston Road

60

59

258

Cha Lodg

Chadstone

Castle
Ashby Lodge

Leys
Close
Dovecote Dr
Grange
Close
The Leys
Fishpond
Fishpond
Cl

Main Street
Church
Orchard La
Surg
Windmill
Lane
Vicarage Lane
By Pass
Way

Denton

Denton
Primary School

Northampton Road
The La
Br Meadow
Denton
Cemy
Wareing Lane
Bedford
Road
Denton Road

Grange Farm

A428

E   F   G   H

84   85

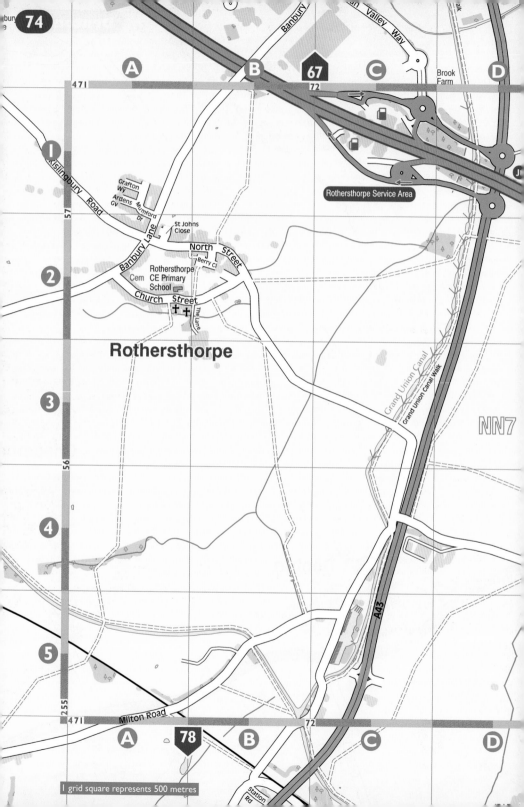

A   B   C   D

471

1

Kislingbury Road

Banbury

Valley Way

Banbury

67
72

Brook Farm

J

Rothersthorpe Service Area

57

Grafton Wy
Ardens Gv
Mumford Dr

St Johns Close

North Street

2

Cem
Berry Cl
Rothersthorpe CE Primary School

Church Street

Rothersthorpe

The Lane

Grand Union Canal

Grand Union Canal Walk

3

56

NN7

4

A43

5

255

471   Milton Road   72

A   78   B   C   D

Station Rd

1 grid square represents 500 metres

East
Hunsbury

Merefield

The Counties
Crematorium

Spring
Farm

Milton
Malsor

Chestnut
Close

Milton Parochial
Primary School

Milton Ct

Maple
Farm

Collingtree Park
Golf Club

Golf Course

Collingtree
Court

Police HQ

Bressingh
Gardens

East Hunsbury
Primary School

Cemetery

E Landimore Road
F Gowerton Road
70
78
G
H
79

Pagnell Court
Hardingstone Lodge
Saucebridge Farm
The Green
I
57

B526
The Green
Mid Greeve
High Greeve
Middle Greeve
Low Greeve
Long Meadow
Lady Hollows Drive
Lordswood Cl
Whittles Cross
Ernstld Cl
Wickman
Thrupp Br
Milton Br
Dene
The Choakles
The Ashes
Pr Lodge Farm
2

B526
Grange Farm
The Grange
3
56

4

Preston Deanery
5
2 55

Preston Deanery Road

E
F
78
G
H
79

Wootton

78

A · B · C · **74** · D

470 · 55 · 71 · Milton Road

Park Lane

Deans Row

St Marys Ct

Station Rd

1

Glebe Farm

PO

PH

Gayton CE Primary School

Works

High Street

Baker Street

Back Lane

Fairfie

Gayton

Hillcrest Rd

Eastcote Rd

2

54

Midshires Way

3

Tiffield Road

Gayton Wilds House

Blisworth Road

A43

Gayton Wood Farm

4

253

Rectory Farm

5

Towc

470 · 71

A · B · C · D

Upper Farm

Woo Cott Farr

Rectory Farm

I grid square represents 500 metres

Tiffield

A   B   C   D

75

I

53

West
Lodge

Courteenhall Road

Courteenhall
Bridge

A508 NORTHAMPTON ROAD

2

Thorpewood
Farm

Wood
Leys Farm

Roade
Cutting

NORTHAMPTON ROAD

3   52

NN7

White House
Farm

ane

Bailey Brooks
La

Northampton

Blisworth Road

Bailey
Brooks
Close

St Mary's Wy

Churchcroft

Bustins La

4

Plain Woods
Farm

Dovecote Road

Priory Crs

Abbots Wy

Hyde Road

Abbey
Road

The Ridings

Hyde Close

London Rd

LONDON ROAD

Orchard Wy

Croft Lane

church End

Surg.

High Stre

PO

Hoe Way

Wallwin Cl

Swale Cl

Grafton Road

The Ridings

The Leys

Hyde
Farm

Works

Roade School
Sports College

Wo

5   251

Way

Midshires

474   75

A   B   C   D

STRATFORD ROAD   A508

E   F   G   H

77   78

I Quinton Green

53

2

3

52

4

5

251

E   F   G   H

77   78

Courteenhall House

Courteenhall

East Lodge

Midshires Way

Fox Covert

Cemetery

Bretts Lane

Fox Covert Dr

The Grove

Hartwell Road

Midshires Way

Ashton Lodge Farm

USING THE STREET INDEX

Street names are listed alphabetically. Each street name is followed by its postal town or area locality, the Postcode District, the page number, and the reference to the square in which the name is found.

Standard index entries are shown as follows:

Abbey Cl *BOZ/IR/WOL* NN29 ....**61** F5

Street names and selected addresses not shown on the map due to scale restrictions are shown in the index with an asterisk:

Beaconsfield Ter *NHTN* NN1 * **55** F3

GENERAL ABBREVIATIONS

ACC	ACCESS	CTYD	COURTYARD	HLS	HILLS	MWY	MOTORWAY	SE	SO
ALY	ALLEY	CUTT	CUTTINGS	HO	HOUSE	N	NORTH	SER	SERV
AP	APPROACH	CV	COVE	HOL	HOLLOW	NE	NORTH EAST	SH	S
AR	ARCADE	CYN	CANYON	HOSP	HOSPITAL	NW	NORTH WEST	SHOP	S
ASS	ASSOCIATION	DEPT	DEPARTMENT	HRB	HARBOUR	O/P	OVERPASS	SKWY	
AV	AVENUE	DL	DALE	HTH	HEATH	OFF	OFFICE	SMT	
BCH	BEACH	DM	DAM	HTS	HEIGHTS	ORCH	ORCHARD	SOC	
BLDS	BUILDINGS	DR	DRIVE	HVN	HAVEN	OV	OVAL	SP	
BND	BEND	DRO	DROVE	HWY	HIGHWAY	PAL	PALACE	SPR	
BNK	BANK	DRY	DRIVEWAY	IMP	IMPERIAL	PAS	PASSAGE	SQ	
BR	BRIDGE	DWGS	DWELLINGS	IN	INLET	PAV	PAVILION	ST	
BRK	BROOK	E	EAST	IND EST	INDUSTRIAL ESTATE	PDE	PARADE	STN	
BTM	BOTTOM	EMB	EMBANKMENT	INF	INFIRMARY	PH	PUBLIC HOUSE	STR	
BUS	BUSINESS	EMBY	EMBASSY	INFO	INFORMATION	PK	PARK	STRD	
BVD	BOULEVARD	ESP	ESPLANADE	INT	INTERCHANGE	PKWY	PARKWAY	SW	SOU
BY	BYPASS	EST	ESTATE	IS	ISLAND	PL	PLACE	TDC	
CATH	CATHEDRAL	EX	EXCHANGE	JCT	JUNCTION	PLN	PLAIN	TER	
CEM	CEMETERY	EXPY	EXPRESSWAY	JTY	JETTY	PLNS	PLAINS	THWY	THRO
CEN	CENTRE	EXT	EXTENSION	KG	KING	PLZ	PLAZA	TNL	
CFT	CROFT	F/O	FLYOVER	KNL	KNOLL	POL	POLICE STATION	TOLL	
CH	CHURCH	FC	FOOTBALL CLUB	L	LAKE	PR	PRINCE	TPK	
CHA	CHASE	FK	FORK	LA	LANE	PREC	PRECINCT	TR	
CHYD	CHURCHYARD	FLD	FIELD	LDG	LODGE	PREP	PREPARATORY	TRL	
CIR	CIRCLE	FLDS	FIELDS	LGT	LIGHT	PRIM	PRIMARY	TWR	
CIRC	CIRCUS	FLS	FALLS	LK	LOCK	PROM	PROMENADE	U/P	UN
CL	CLOSE	FM	FARM	LKS	LAKES	PRS	PRINCESS	UNI	UN
CLFS	CLIFFS	FT	FORT	LNDG	LANDING	PRT	PORT	UPR	
CMP	CAMP	FTS	FLATS	LTL	LITTLE	PT	POINT	V	
CNR	CORNER	FWY	FREEWAY	LWR	LOWER	PTH	PATH	VA	
CO	COUNTY	GA	GATE	MAG	MAGISTRATE	PZ	PIAZZA	VIAD	
COLL	COLLEGE	GAL	GALLERY	MAN	MANSIONS	QD	QUADRANT	VIL	
COM	COMMON	GDN	GARDEN	MD	MEAD	QU	QUEEN	VIS	
COMM	COMMISSION	GDNS	GARDENS	MDW	MEADOWS	QY	QUAY	VLG	
CON	CONVENT	GLD	GLADE	MEM	MEMORIAL	R	RIVER	VLS	
COT	COTTAGE	GLN	GLEN	MI	MILL	RBT	ROUNDABOUT	VW	
COTS	COTTAGES	GN	GREEN	MKT	MARKET	RD	ROAD	W	WD
CP	CAPE	GND	GROUND	MKTS	MARKETS	RDG	RIDGE	WD	
CPS	COPSE	GRA	GRANGE	ML	MALL	REP	REPUBLIC	WHF	
CR	CREEK	GRG	GARAGE	MNR	MANOR	RES	RESERVOIR	WK	
CREM	CREMATORIUM	GT	GREAT	MS	MEWS	RFC	RUGBY FOOTBALL CLUB	WKS	
CRS	CRESCENT	GTWY	GATEWAY	MSN	MISSION	RI	RISE	WLS	
CSWY	CAUSEWAY	GV	GROVE	MT	MOUNT	RM	RAMP	WY	
CT	COURT	HGR	HIGHER	MTN	MOUNTAIN	RW	ROW	YD	
CTRL	CENTRAL	HL	HILL	MTS	MOUNTAINS	S	SOUTH	YHA	YOUTH
CTS	COURTS			MUS	MUSEUM	SCH	SCHOOL		

POSTCODE TOWNS AND AREA ABBREVIATIONS

BOZ/IR/WOL	Bozeat/Irchester/Wollaston	DAV	Daventry	NHTNE/MOU	Northampton east/Moulton	NHTNS	Northampton south
BRIX/LBKBY	Brixworth/Long Buckby	IR/RAU/FIN	Irthlingborough/Raunds/Finedon	NHTNN/BOU	Northampton north/Boughton	NHTNW	Northampton west
		NHTN	Northampton			RNHPTN	Rural Northampton
						RSHD/HF	F
						TOW	Highar, Te
						WBORO	Welling

A

		Abington Park Crs *NHTNE/MOU* NN3	56 C3	**Adnitt Rd** *NHTN* NN1	55 H3
		Abington Sq *NHTN* NN1	3 G2	*RSHD/HF* NN10	33 E2
		Abington St *NHTN* NN1	3 F2	**Affleck Br** *IR/RAU/FIN* NN9	7 H2
Abbey Cl *BOZ/IR/WOL* NN29	61 F5	**Abthorpe Av** *NHTNN/BOU* NN2	41 F2	**Aggate Wy** *BRIX/LBKBY* NN6	45 H4
Abbey Ri *BOZ/IR/WOL* NN29	48 D2	**Ace La** *RNHPTN* NN7	65 F5	**Agnes Rd** *NHTNN/BOU* NN2	55 E2
Abbey Rd *NHTNS* NN4	68 D2	**Acorn Cl** *NHTNW* NN5	53 E3	**Ainsdale Cl** *NHTNN/BOU* NN2	41 H4
RNHPTN NN7	80 C4	**Acre Cl** *DAV* NN11	55 E5	**Aintree Dr** *RSHD/HF* NN10	33 H4
WBORO NN8	29 H1	**Acre La** *NHTNN/BOU* NN2	40 C2	**Aintree Rd** *NHTNE/MOU* NN5	41 H3
Abbey St *DAV* NN11	51 E2	**Adams Av** *NHTN* NN1	55 H3	**Albany Rd** *NHTN* NN1	56 A3
NHTNW NN5	54 C4	**Adams Cl** *IR/RAU/FIN* NN9	10 C5	**Albert Pl** *NHTN* NN1	2 E2
Abbey Wy *RSHD/HF* NN10	33 E4	*WBORO* NN8	16 B4	**Albert Rd** *IR/RAU/FIN* NN9	7 H1
Abbot Cl *DAV* NN11	51 F4	**Addington Rd** *IR/RAU/FIN* NN9	9 F4	*RSHD/HF* NN10	33 J3
Abbots Wy *NHTNW* NN5	54 B4	**Addison Rd** *NHTNE/MOU* NN3	42 A5	*WBORO* NN8	16 B4
RNHPTN NN7	80 D5	**Addlecroft Cl**		**Albion Pl** *NHTN* NN1	1 E4
WBORO NN8	15 H5	*NHTNN/BOU* NN2	40 D4	*RSHD/HF* NN10	33 F3
Abbotts Wy *RSHD/HF* NN10	32 D3	**Adelaide St** *NHTNN/BOU* NN2	55 E3	**Alcombe Rd** *NHTN* NN1	3 F2
Aberdare Rd *NHTNW* NN5	54 C2	**Adit Vw** *IR/RAU/FIN* NN9	18 B1	**Alcombe Ter** *NHTN* NN1	3 G1
Abington Av *NHTN* NN1	55 H2	**Admirals Wy** *DAV* NN11	51 G4	**Alder Ct** *NHTNE/MOU* NN5	43 F2
				Aderley Cl *NHTNW* NN5	53 F2

Aidsworth Cl *WBORO* NN8	29 G4	**Allen Rd** *IR/RAU/FIN* NN9
Aldwell Cl *NHTNS* NN4	76 D2	*NHTN* NN1
Alexander Ct		*RSHD/HF* NN10
NHTNE/MOU NN3	43 E4	**Allens Hl** *BOZ/IR/WOL* NN29
Alexander Pl *IR/RAU/FIN* NN9	9 G2	**Alliance Ter** *WBORO* NN8
Alexander Rd *NHTN* NN1	3 G3	**Alliston Gdns**
Alexandra Rd *NHTN* NN1	3 G3	*NHTNN/BOU* NN2
RSHD/HF NN10	33 H2	**Alma St** *NHTNW* NN5
WBORO NN8	16 B4	*WBORO* NN8
Alfred St *BOZ/IR/WOL* NN29	31 C4	**Almond Crs** *RNHPTN* NN7
IR/RAU/FIN NN9	10 B4	**Alpine Cl** *RSHD/HF* NN10
NHTN NN1	3 J3	**Alpine Wy** *NHTNW* NN5
RSHD/HF NN10	33 F2	**Alsace Cl** *NHTNW* NN5
Allbone Cl *NHTNE/MOU* NN3	24 D5	**Althorp Cl** *WBORO* NN8
Alington Cl *IR/RAU/FIN* NN9	8 A1	**Althorp Rd** *NHTNW* NN5
Alken Cl *WBORO* NN8	15 H1	**Althorp St** *NHTN* NN1
Allard Cl *NHTNE/MOU* NN5	44 B2	**Alton St** *NHTNS* NN4
Allebone Rd *BRIX/LBKBY* NN6	46 A4	**Alvis Ct** *NHTNE/MOU* NN5
Allen Ct *IR/RAU/FIN* NN9	8 A1	**Alvis Wy** *DAV* NN11

de Cl NHTNE/MOU NN3 ... 42 C3
O NN8 ... 15 E4
e Cl NHTNS NN4 ... 68 B5
St NHTNW NN5 ... 54 C4
en Cl DAV NN11 ... 34 D4
Dr NHTNN/BOU NN2 ... 40 D1
Cl RSHD/HF NN10 ... 19 G2
s Wy IR/RAU/FIN NN9 ... 10 D3
WBORO NN8 ... 16 A5
NHTN NN1 ... 2 D4
Rd DAV NN11 ... 50 D3
y NHTNE/MOU NN3 ... 41 H1
NHTNW NN5 ... 38 D5
RSHD/HF NN10 ... 19 G2
WBORO NN8 ... 29 G2
y Cl NHTNE/MOU NN3 ... 56 D4
y NHTNS NN4 ... 69 F5
DAV NN11 ... 51 F3
Cl IR/RAU/FIN NN9 ... 10 D4
Dr IR/RAU/FIN NN9 ... 10 D4
Gdns IR/RAU/FIN NN9 ... 10 D4
RNHPTN NN7 ... 65 F5
DAV NN11 ... 50 D1
Cl IR/RAU/FIN NN9 ... 6 B5
re Cl NHTNN/BOU NN2 ... 41 E3
roach NHTNW NN5 ... 54 B4
e Cl NHTNW NN5 ... 52 D1
t NHTNE/MOU NN3 ... 43 E3
iew Ct
E/MOU NN3 ... 43 E3
el Rd NHTNS NN4 ... 68 A3
el Sq NHTNS NN4 ... 68 B3
Cl NHTNN/BOU NN2 ... 40 D2
d WBORO NN8 ... 15 H5
DAV NN11 ... 34 D5
v RNHPTN NN7 ... 74 A1
n Rd NHTN NN1 ... 56 A3
NHTNW NN5 ... 54 B4
HTNW NN5 ... 53 E1
nt Rd
R/WOL NN29 ... 31 H4
Rd NHTNE/MOU NN3 ... 43 G3
NHTNN/BOU NN2 ... 40 B2
d NHTNN/BOU NN2 ... 55 E2
rs NHTNE/MOU NN3 ... 24 B3
s DAV NN11 ... 34 D5
ead Rd NHTNS NN4 ... 68 B2
NHTNN/BOU NN2 ... 55 E1
O NN8 ... 15 G5
RSHD/HF NN10 ... 33 G5
Ct RSHD/HF NN10 ... 33 E4
St NHTN NN1 ... 2 C1
RSHD/HF NN10 ... 33 H4
Rd NHTNS NN4 ... 68 B2
ham Rd NHTN NN1 ... 55 H2
WBORO NN8 ... 15 F2
NHTNE/MOU NN3 ... 24 C3
N NN7 ... 66 B2
RSHD/HF NN10 ... 33 E4
dns NHTNE/MOU NN3 ... 24 C3
DAV NN11 ... 34 D5
d DAV NN11 ... 34 D5
OZ/IR/WOL NN29 ... 31 G5
N11 ... 35 E5
Cl NHTNW NN5 ... 53 F1
Gdns
E/MOU NN3 ... 42 A5
Cl BRIX/LBKBY NN6 ... 26 B3
n Rd DAV NN11 ... 35 E5
RIX/LBKBY NN6 ... 26 B5
s NHTNS NN4 ... 77 F2
TN NN7 ... 65 F5
Av IR/RAU/FIN NN9 ... 11 E2
Ri IR/RAU/FIN NN9 ... 11 E2
Rd WBORO NN8 ... 15 G5
Cl NHTNE/MOU NN3 ... 56 C4
HTNN/BOU NN2 ... 40 D1
N NN7 ... 65 F5
HTNS NN4 ... 75 H4
RNHPTN NN7 ... 79 F4
NHTNE/MOU NN3 ... 24 D3
y NHTNE/MOU NN3 ... 42 D5
NHTNE/MOU NN3 ... 43 G5
Spinney NHTNS NN4 ... 67 G3
Cl RSHD/HF NN10 ... 33 E4
HTNN/BOU NN2 ... 41 E1
HTN NN1 ... 2 D1
DAV NN11 ... 50 C1
v WBORO NN8 ... 15 F1
d RNHPTN NN7 ... 80 D5
Wy NHTNW NN5 ... 53 G3
vay BRIX/LBKBY NN6 ... 5 E5
LBKBY NN6 ... 12 D1
Rd RSHD/HF NN10 ... 33 H2
Rd NHTNW NN5 ... 53 G3
n St DAV NN11 ... 51 E3
Av WBORO NN8 ... 29 G3
NHTNE/MOU NN3 ... 44 A4
HF NN10 ... 33 F1
Cl DAV NN11 ... 51 E4
NHTNE/MOU NN3 ... 56 D4
NHTNW NN5 ... 53 F2
y Wy NHTNS NN4 ... 71 F3
NHTNE/MOU NN3 ... 42 B3
WBORO NN8 ... 15 E4
IR/RAU/FIN NN9 ... 9 G3
Cl NHTNN/BOU NN2 ... 41 F5
ers Wy NHTN NN1 ... 2 E6
Av NHTNS NN4 ... 75 H2
BOZ/IR/WOL NN29 ... 32 A4
NHTN NN1 ... 55 F3
y DAV NN11 ... 50 B1
Wy NHTNS NN4 ... 68 D5
Cl IR/RAU/FIN NN9 ... 7 G1
Rd IR/RAU/FIN NN9 ... 7 G1
O NN8 ... 16 A4
ue IR/RAU/FIN NN9 ... 10 C5
NN1 ... 3 J4
E/MOU NN3 ... 42 A4
/BOU NN2 ... 40 B1
W NN5 ... 54 B3
TN NN7 ... 63 G3
O NN8 ... 16 A3
e Gdns NHTNS NN4 ... 68 A4
Cl NHTNW NN5 ... 39 E5
DAV NN11 ... 50 C3
O NN8 ... 15 E3
NHTNW NN5 ... 54 A1
d Rd NHTNS NN4 ... 68 B1
's NHTNN/BOU NN2 ... 41 E2
Aynho Wk NHTNN/BOU NN2 ... 41 E2
Azalea Cl NHTNE/MOU NN3 ... 56 D4

B

Back La BRIX/LBKBY NN6 ... 5 H1
BRIX/LBKBY NN6 ... 21 H3
NHTNS NN4 ... 69 H5
RNHPTN NN7 ... 36 D3
RNHPTN NN7 ... 78 A1
Backway BOZ/IR/WOL NN29 ... 48 D3
Bacon Rd WBORO NN8 ... 15 G1
Badby Cl NHTNN/BOU NN2 ... 41 G3
Badby Pk DAV NN11 ... 34 C4
Badby Rd DAV NN11 ... 50 D4
Badby Rd West DAV NN11 ... 50 C5
Badger La NHTNS NN4 ... 76 D5
Badgers Cl RNHPTN NN7 ... 65 F5
Badgers Wk NHTNN/BOU NN2 ... 40 D2
Bailey Brooks Cl RNHPTN NN7 ... 80 C4
Bailey Brooks La RNHPTN NN7 ... 80 C3
Bailey Ct RSHD/HF NN10 ... 19 F4
Bailiff St NHTN NN1 ... 55 F3
Baines Wy NHTNS NN4 ... 76 C5
Baird Av NHTNW NN5 ... 67 H1
Baird Cl DAV NN11 ... 34 D4
Baird Ct WBORO NN8 ... 14 D3
Bakehouse La BRIX/LBKBY NN6 ... 27 F2
Bakers Crs BOZ/IR/WOL NN29 ... 31 G4
Baker St IR/RAU/FIN NN9 ... 9 E5
NHTNN/BOU NN2 ... 54 D2
RNHPTN NN7 ... 78 A1
WBORO NN8 ... 16 A4
Bakewell Cl NHTNS NN4 ... 68 B5
Baldwin Cl NHTNE/MOU NN3 ... 42 C3
Baler Cl DAV NN11 ... 35 E3
Balfour Rd NHTNN/BOU NN2 ... 55 E1
Balham Cl RSHD/HF NN10 ... 32 D4
Balland Wy NHTNS NN4 ... 76 D1
Ballantyne Rd RSHD/HF NN10 ... 33 E3
Balliol Rd DAV NN11 ... 50 D4
Balmoral Av RSHD/HF NN10 ... 33 G1
Balmoral Cl BRIX/LBKBY NN6 ... 46 B4
WBORO NN8 ... 29 G3
Balmoral Rd NHTNN/BOU NN2 ... 55 E1
Banbury Cl NHTNS NN4 ... 67 H4
WBORO NN8 ... 29 G3
Banbury La NHTNS NN4 ... 67 F5
RNHPTN NN7 ... 74 A2
Bancroft Cl NHTNS NN4 ... 76 D2
Bancroft Wy NHTNS NN4 ... 76 D3
Bankside NHTNN/BOU NN2 ... 41 H4
RSHD/HF NN10 ... 19 F2
The Banks IR/RAU/FIN NN9 ... 15 H1
Bank Vw NHTNS NN4 ... 75 H1
Bants La NHTNW NN5 ... 54 A3
Baptists Cl RNHPTN NN7 ... 65 F5
Baring Rd NHTNW NN5 ... 54 C3
Barker Cl RSHD/HF NN10 ... 33 F2
Barker Rd BRIX/LBKBY NN6 ... 46 A4
Barley Cl DAV NN11 ... 35 E3
Barley Ct RSHD/HF NN10 ... 33 G4
Barley Hill Rd
NHTNE/MOU NN3 ... 43 G1
Barley La NHTNN/BOU NN2 ... 40 D2
Barlow La NHTNE/MOU NN3 ... 24 C3
Barnard Cl NHTNW NN5 ... 53 F2
Barn Cl NHTNS NN4 ... 76 D5
Barn Cnr NHTNS NN4 ... 76 A4
Barnes Cl DAV NN11 ... 50 D1
Barneswell Cl BRIX/LBKBY NN6 ... 4 D4
Barnet Cl NHTNS NN4 ... 68 C4
Barnfield Cl NHTNN/BOU NN2 ... 40 D3
Barnhill Sq NHTNE/MOU NN3 ... 43 G1
Barn La RNHPTN NN7 ... 75 F5
Barn Ms NHTNS NN4 ... 76 A4
Barn Owl Cl NHTNS NN4 ... 68 C5
Barnstaple Cl
NHTNE/MOU NN3 ... 57 E3
Barn Wy NHTNW NN5 ... 39 F4
Barnwell Dr RSHD/HF NN10 ... 33 E4
Barnwell Gdns WBORO NN8 ... 15 F2
Barnwell Rd NHTNN/BOU NN2 ... 41 F3
WBORO NN8 ... 15 F2
Baron Av BRIX/LBKBY NN6 ... 46 B2
Baronson Gdns NHTN NN1 ... 55 H2
Barons Wy NHTNN/BOU NN2 ... 40 C3
Barrack Rd NHTN NN1 ... 2 D1
Barratt Cl RSHD/HF NN10 ... 19 F4
Barringers Gdns
BOZ/IR/WOL NN29 ... 31 G3
Barrington Rd RSHD/HF NN10 ... 33 H3
Barry Rd NHTN NN1 ... 56 A4
Barton Flds BRIX/LBKBY NN6 ... 44 D4
The Bartons Cl NHTNW NN5 ... 54 B1
Basil Cl NHTNS NN4 ... 76 B2
Bates Cl RSHD/HF NN10 ... 19 F4
Batsmans Dr RSHD/HF NN10 ... 19 E5
Battalion Dr NHTNS NN4 ... 76 C2
Battle Cl NHTNS NN4 ... 76 B1
Baulmsholme Cl NHTNS NN4 ... 2 C7
Baunhill Cl NHTNE/MOU NN3 ... 56 D3
Baxter Ct NHTNS NN4 ... 69 H5
Beacon Ct NHTNS NN4 ... 68 A2
Beaconsfield Pl RSHD/HF NN10 ... 33 F1
Beaconsfield Ter NHTN NN1 * ... 55 F3
Beatty Cl DAV NN11 ... 51 G3
Beaufort Dr NHTNW NN5 ... 53 G1
Beaumaris Cl RSHD/HF NN10 ... 33 G3
Beaumont Ct NHTN NN1 ... 2 C2
Beaumont Dr
NHTNE/MOU NN3 ... 43 H4
Beaune Cl NHTNW NN5 ... 52 D1
Beauvais Ct NHTNW NN5 ... 52 D1
Beck Ct WBORO NN8 ... 15 F3
Beckets Vw NHTN NN1 ... 3 G5
Becket Wy NHTNE/MOU NN3 ... 42 B2
Bective Rd NHTNN/BOU NN2 ... 41 E4
Bective Vw NHTNN/BOU NN2 ... 41 F3
Bedale Rd WBORO NN8 ... 16 A4
Beddoes Cl NHTNS NN4 ... 77 E2
Bede Cl RSHD/HF NN10 ... 19 G4
Bedford Pl NHTN NN1 ... 3 F4
Bedford Rd NHTN NN1 ... 3 G5
NHTNS NN4 ... 70 A1
RSHD/HF NN10 ... 33 G5
Beech Av NHTNE/MOU NN3 ... 56 A1
Beech Cl RNHPTN NN7 ... 65 F5
Beech Crs BOZ/IR/WOL NN29 ... 31 G5
Beechcroft Gdns
NHTNE/MOU NN3 ... 42 A5
Beech Dr WBORO NN8 ... 15 G4
Beech Gv NHTNE/MOU NN3 ... 42 D2
RSHD/HF NN10 ... 32 D1
Beech La RNHPTN NN7 ... 66 C1
Beech Rd RSHD/HF NN10 ... 19 F5
Beechwood Dr
NHTNE/MOU NN3 ... 57 E1
Beechwood Rd NHTNW NN5 ... 53 G3
Beeston Av NHTNE/MOU NN3 ... 57 F2
Belfry La NHTNS NN4 ... 75 H3
Belfry Wy DAV NN11 ... 51 G2
Bell End BOZ/IR/WOL NN29 ... 48 D3
Bell Hl IR/RAU/FIN NN9 ... 7 G2
Bellropes Sq NHTNE/MOU NN3 ... 44 B5
Bell St WBORO NN8 ... 16 A4
Belmont Gdns IR/RAU/FIN NN9 ... 11 E2
Belstead Rd NHTNE/MOU NN3 ... 56 D4
Belton Cl NHTNS NN4 ... 69 E5
Belvedere Cl NHTNW NN5 ... 54 B3
Belvoir Cl NHTNW NN5 ... 53 F1
RSHD/HF NN10 ... 33 G3
Bembridge Dr
NHTNN/BOU NN2 ... 54 D1
Benbow Cl DAV NN11 ... 51 G2
Benedict Cl RSHD/HF NN10 ... 32 D4
Benjamin Sq NHTNS NN4 ... 68 B3
Bentley Cl NHTNE/MOU NN3 ... 44 B3
Bentley Ct WBORO NN8 ... 6 D5
Bentley Wy DAV NN11 ... 50 B1
Bergerac Cl NHTNW NN5 ... 38 D5
Berkeley Cl NHTN NN1 ... 3 J3
Bern Links NHTNS NN4 ... 68 B2
Bern Side NHTNS NN4 ... 68 C2
Berrill St BOZ/IR/WOL NN29 ... 31 G5
Berrister Pl IR/RAU/FIN NN9 ... 11 G1
Berry Cl BRIX/LBKBY NN6 ... 46 A2
RNHPTN NN7 ... 74 B2
Berrydale NHTNE/MOU NN3 ... 44 B4
Berry Green Rd IR/RAU/FIN NN9 ... 7 G1
Berry La NHTNS NN4 ... 76 B3
Berrymoor Rd WBORO NN8 ... 29 G3
Berrywood Cl NHTNW NN5 ... 53 E3
Berrywood Dr NHTNW NN5 ... 52 D3
Berrywood Rd NHTNW NN5 ... 52 D2
Bestwell Ct NHTNE/MOU NN3 ... 57 G2
Betjeman Cl DAV NN11 ... 50 C1
RSHD/HF NN10 ... 19 E4
Betony Wk RSHD/HF NN10 ... 33 F4
Bevan Cl WBORO NN8 ... 16 C2
Beverley Crs NHTNE/MOU NN3 ... 42 B5
Bewick Rd NHTNE/MOU NN3 ... 57 E3
Bibury Cl WBORO NN8 ... 29 F3
Bibury Crs NHTNE/MOU NN3 ... 42 D2
Bidders Cl NHTN NN1 ... 2 E6
Bideford Cl NHTNE/MOU NN3 ... 56 D3
Billing Brook Rd
NHTNE/MOU NN3 ... 42 D2
Billing La BRIX/LBKBY NN6 ... 25 F4
NHTNE/MOU NN3 ... 43 G1
Billing Rd NHTN NN1 ... 3 G3
RNHPTN NN7 ... 72 B1
Billing Rd East
NHTNE/MOU NN3 ... 56 C4
Billing School Pl RNHPTN NN7 ... 63 E4
Billington St NHTN NN1 ... 3 J1
Bilsdon Cl RSHD/HF NN10 ... 32 D4
Binder Cl RSHD/HF NN10 ... 19 E2
Birchall Rd RSHD/HF NN10 ... 32 D2
Birch Barn Wy
NHTNN/BOU NN2 ... 40 D2
Birchfield Crs
NHTNE/MOU NN3 ... 42 C5
Birchfield Rd NHTN NN1 ... 55 H2
WBORO NN8 ... 15 F5
Birchfield Rd East
NHTNE/MOU NN3 ... 56 A1
Birch Rd RSHD/HF NN10 ... 33 G2
Birds Hill Rd NHTNE/MOU NN3 ... 43 G4
Birds Hill Wk NHTNE/MOU NN3 ... 43 F5
Birkdale Cl DAV NN11 ... 51 G2
NHTNN/BOU NN2 ... 41 H4
Birkdale Dr RSHD/HF NN10 ... 33 H3
Bishops Dr NHTNN/BOU NN2 ... 40 D4
Bitten Ct NHTNE/MOU NN3 ... 43 E4
Blackberry La NHTNS NN4 ... 68 B2
Black Cat Dr NHTNW NN5 ... 67 H1
Blackfriars RSHD/HF NN10 ... 32 D3
Black Lion Hl NHTN NN1 ... 2 A4
Blacksmiths La RNHPTN NN7 ... 36 B5
Blackthorn Bridge Ct
NHTNE/MOU NN3 ... 43 H3
Blackthorn Rd
NHTNE/MOU NN3 ... 43 H3
Blackwall Cl NHTNS NN4 ... 68 C3
Blackwell Cl BRIX/LBKBY NN6 ... 46 A3
RSHD/HF NN10 ... 19 E1
Blackwell Hl NHTNS NN4 ... 68 B5
Blackymore La NHTNS NN4 ... 76 B3
Bladon Cl NHTNE/MOU NN3 ... 42 C3
Blake Cl DAV NN11 ... 51 G4
Blakesley Cl NHTNN/BOU NN2 ... 41 E2
Blake Wk RSHD/HF NN10 ... 19 E4
Blanchard Cl NHTNS NN4 ... 76 C1
Bledlow Ri NHTNS NN4 ... 68 B5
Blenheim Cl RSHD/HF NN10 ... 33 E4
Blenheim Rd NHTNS NN4 ... 68 D3
WBORO NN8 ... 15 F2
Blinco Rd RSHD/HF NN10 ... 33 G2
Bliss La RNHPTN NN7 ... 63 H2
Blisworth Cl NHTNS NN4 ... 68 C3
Blisworth Rd RNHPTN NN7 ... 78 C3
RNHPTN NN7 ... 80 B4
Bloomfield Cl RSHD/HF NN10 ... 32 D2
Blossac Ct NHTNW NN5 ... 52 D1
Blossom Wy NHTNE/MOU NN3 ... 57 G1
Bluebell Cl WBORO NN8 ... 16 B3
Bluebell Ct NHTNE/MOU NN3 ... 56 C4
Bluebell Ri RSHD/HF NN10 ... 33 G4
Blueberry Ri NHTNE/MOU NN3 ... 44 A5
Boarden Cl NHTNE/MOU NN3 ... 24 A5
Board St IR/RAU/FIN NN9 ... 9 F4
Bobtail Ct NHTNW NN5 ... 53 G1
Bodleian Cl DAV NN11 ... 50 D4
Bolingbroke Pl RSHD/HF NN10 ... 19 G1
Bollinger Cl NHTNW NN5 ... 52 D1
Bondfield Av NHTNN/BOU NN2 ... 41 F4
Booth Dr WBORO NN8 ... 14 C5
Booth La North
NHTNE/MOU NN3 ... 42 C3
Booth La South
NHTNE/MOU NN3 ... 42 D4
Booth Meadow Ct
NHTNE/MOU NN3 ... 43 E2
Booth Ri NHTNE/MOU NN3 ... 42 C1
Bordeaux Cl NHTNW NN5 ... 52 D1
Borough Ct RSHD/HF NN10 ... 19 F4
Borrowdale Wk
NHTNE/MOU NN3 ... 42 C3
Bostock Av NHTN NN1 ... 55 H3
Bostock Ms NHTN NN1 ... 3 K1
Bosworth Cl NHTNS NN4 ... 68 C4
Botmead Rd NHTNE/MOU NN3 ... 44 B3
Bougainvillea Dr
NHTNE/MOU NN3 ... 56 C4
Boughton Dr RSHD/HF NN10 ... 33 E4
Boughton Fair La
NHTNE/MOU NN3 ... 24 B1
Boughton Green Rd
NHTNE/MOU NN3 ... 23 G5
NHTNN/BOU NN2 ... 41 F2
Boughton La NHTNE/MOU NN3 ... 42 B1
Boughton Rd
NHTNE/MOU NN3 ... 24 A3
Boundary Av RSHD/HF NN10 ... 32 C2
Bourne Cl WBORO NN8 ... 15 E3
Bourne Crs NHTNW NN5 ... 54 A1
Bourton Cl NHTNS NN4 ... 68 A5
Bourton Wy WBORO NN8 ... 29 G4
Bouverie Rd NHTNS NN4 ... 69 G5
Bouverie St NHTN NN1 ... 3 J2
Bouverie Wk NHTN NN1 ... 3 J2
Bow Ct NHTNS NN4 ... 68 A2
Bowden Rd NHTNW NN5 ... 54 C4
Bowling Green La NHTNW NN5 ... 53 E4
Bowmans Cl NHTNS NN4 ... 67 H4
Bowness WBORO NN8 ... 15 E4
Bowthorpe Cl
NHTNE/MOU NN3 ... 56 D4
Bracken Borough
BRIX/LBKBY NN6 ... 5 E5
Bracken Field Sq
NHTNE/MOU NN3 ... 25 F5
Brackenhill Cl
NHTNN/BOU NN2 ... 41 G4
Brackley Cl NHTNN/BOU NN2 ... 41 F2
Bradden Cl NHTNN/BOU NN2 ... 41 F2
Bradfield Cl RSHD/HF NN10 ... 33 H1
WBORO NN8 ... 6 C5
Bradfield Rd WBORO NN8 ... 6 C5
Bradmoor Ct NHTNE/MOU NN3 ... 43 H2
Bradshaw St NHTN NN1 ... 2 D3
Bradshaw Wy
BOZ/IR/WOL NN29 ... 31 F4
Brad St NHTNE/MOU NN3 ... 42 B2
Braemar Crs NHTNS NN4 ... 68 D5
Brafield Rd RNHPTN NN7 ... 72 B1
Braid Ct WBORO NN8 ... 15 F2
Bramble End NHTNS NN4 ... 68 B5
Bramcote Dr NHTNE/MOU NN3 ... 57 F2
Bramhall Ri NHTNW NN5 ... 53 F2
Bramley Cl RNHPTN NN7 ... 58 C4
RSHD/HF NN10 ... 32 D1
Bramley Ct BOZ/IR/WOL NN29 ... 48 D2
Bramley Gv NHTNE/MOU NN3 ... 43 H5
Brampton Cl WBORO NN8 ... 15 F2
Brampton La BRIX/LBKBY NN6 ... 22 B1
Brampton Wk
NHTNE/MOU NN3 ... 41 H2
Brampton Wy BRIX/LBKBY NN6 ... 4 D4
Branksome Av
NHTNN/BOU NN2 ... 54 D1
Brashland Dr NHTNS NN4 ... 76 B2
Braunston Rd DAV NN11 ... 34 A4
Brawn Cl IR/RAU/FIN NN9 ... 18 C1
Brayford Cl NHTNE/MOU NN3 ... 56 C3
Breach Cl BRIX/LBKBY NN6 ... 5 E4
Brecon St NHTNW NN5 ... 54 C2
Breezehill NHTNS NN4 ... 76 C2
Brembridge Cl
BRIX/LBKBY NN6 ... 26 B2
Brendon Cl NHTNE/MOU NN3 ... 56 D3
Brer Ct NHTNS NN4 ... 3 K5
Bressingham Gdns NHTNS NN4 ... 76 A1
Bretton Cl NHTNW NN5 ... 53 E1
Bretts La RNHPTN NN7 ... 81 E4
Briar Ct IR/RAU/FIN NN9 ... 9 F4
Briar Hill Rd NHTNS NN4 ... 68 D3
Briar Hill Wk NHTNS NN4 ... 68 D3
Briarwood Wy
BOZ/IR/WOL NN29 ... 48 D4
Brickett's La RNHPTN NN7 ... 63 G2
Brickhill Rd WBORO NN8 ... 15 F5
Brick Kiln La NHTNN/BOU NN2 ... 55 E2
Brickwell Ct NHTNE/MOU NN3 ... 57 G1
Brickyard Spinney Rd
NHTNE/MOU NN3 ... 42 B1
Bridge Meadow RNHPTN NN7 ... 73 F5
Bridge Meadow Wy
NHTNS NN4 ... 76 D5
Bridge St IR/RAU/FIN NN9 ... 11 F1
NHTN NN1 ... 2 D5
RNHPTN NN7 ... 62 D4
Bridgewater Dr
NHTNE/MOU NN3 ... 56 C3
Bridle Cl RNHPTN NN7 ... 72 B3
WBORO NN8 ... 6 C5
Brigadier Cl NHTNS NN4 ... 76 B1
Brightwell Wk
IR/RAU/FIN NN9 ... 18 B1
Brindlestone Cl NHTNS NN4 ... 67 H3
Brindley Cl DAV NN11 ... 34 B4
RSHD/HF NN10 ... 18 D5
Briscoe Cl NHTNN/BOU NN2 ... 41 G1
Bristle St NHTNW NN5 ... 67 G1
Britannia Gdns WBORO NN8 ... 16 C5
Briton Gdns NHTNE/MOU NN3 ... 56 B1
Briton Rd NHTNE/MOU NN3 ... 56 B2
Briton Ter NHTNE/MOU NN3 ... 56 B1
Brittons Dr NHTNE/MOU NN3 ... 25 G5
Brixworth Hall Pk
BRIX/LBKBY NN6 ... 4 D3
Brixworth Rd BRIX/LBKBY NN6 ... 4 A4
Broadhurst Dr
NHTNE/MOU NN3 ... 57 F2
Broadlands BRIX/LBKBY NN6 ... 4 C5
IR/RAU/FIN NN9 ... 11 G2
Broad March DAV NN11 ... 51 F4
Broadmead Av
NHTNE/MOU NN3 ... 42 A5
Broad St BRIX/LBKBY NN6 ... 4 D5
BRIX/LBKBY NN6 ... 46 A3
NHTN NN1 ... 2 C2
Broadway NHTN NN1 ... 56 A1
WBORO NN8 ... 30 A1
Broadway East
NHTNE/MOU NN3 ... 56 B1
Brocade Cl NHTNS NN4 ... 68 B3
Brockhall Cl NHTNN/BOU NN2 ... 41 G3
Brockhall Rd NHTNN/BOU NN2 ... 41 G3
RNHPTN NN7 ... 63 G1
Brockton St NHTNN/BOU NN2 ... 55 F1
Brockwood Cl NHTNW NN5 ... 53 E1
Bromford Cl NHTNE/MOU NN3 ... 57 G2
Brooke Cl RSHD/HF NN10 ... 33 F3
WBORO NN8 ... 14 D4
Brookend NHTNS NN4 ... 76 C3
Brookfield Rd
NHTNN/BOU NN2 ... 41 G5
RSHD/HF NN10 ... 33 E2
Brookland Crs NHTN NN1 ... 56 A1
Brookland Rd NHTN NN1 ... 55 H1
Brooklands Cl DAV NN11 ... 51 E3
Brook La NHTNW NN5 ... 54 B2
Brookside BOZ/IR/WOL NN29 ... 61 G5
IR/RAU/FIN NN9 ... 10 C5
RNHPTN NN7 ... 62 D4
Brookside Mdw NHTNW NN5 ... 54 A1
Brookside Pl RNHPTN NN7 ... 64 C2
Brooks Rd IR/RAU/FIN NN9 ... 11 G1
Brook St DAV NN11 ... 50 D2
IR/RAU/FIN NN9 ... 11 F2
NHTN NN1 ... 2 B1
Brook St East WBORO NN8 ... 16 B5
Brook St West WBORO NN8 ... 15 G5
Brook V WBORO NN8 ... 29 E3
Brook Vw NHTNS NN4 ... 76 C5
Broomhill Crs
NHTNE/MOU NN3 ... 43 G1
Brough Cl NHTNW NN5 ... 52 D1
Broughton Pl
NHTNE/MOU NN3 ... 42 B4
Browning Cl DAV NN11 ... 34 D5
RSHD/HF NN10 ... 33 H4
Browning Rd WBORO NN8 ... 15 E5
Brownlow Ct NHTNE/MOU NN3 ... 43 E3
Browns Cl NHTNE/MOU NN3 ... 24 D2
Browns Rd DAV NN11 ... 50 A3
Brown's Wy NHTN NN1 ... 3 H5
Browns Yd RNHPTN NN7 ... 65 F5
Bruce St NHTNW NN5 ... 54 B4
Brundall Cl NHTNE/MOU NN3 ... 56 D3
Brunel Cl DAV NN11 ... 34 B5
WBORO NN8 ... 14 D3
Brunel Dr NHTNW NN5 ... 67 G1
Brunswick Pl NHTN NN1 ... 3 H1
Brunswick Wk NHTN NN1 ... 3 H1
Brunting Rd NHTNE/MOU NN3 ... 24 C4
Bryant Wy RSHD/HF NN10 ... 19 F3
Buchanan Cl NHTNS NN4 ... 68 C3
Buckingham Cl NHTNS NN4 ... 75 H1
WBORO NN8 ... 29 G3
Buckwell Cl WBORO NN8 ... 15 H4
Buckwell End WBORO NN8 ... 15 H4
Bugbrooke Rd RNHPTN NN7 ... 64 C3
RNHPTN NN7 ... 66 A3
Bugby Dr IR/RAU/FIN NN9 ... 9 H1
Bugby Wy IR/RAU/FIN NN9 ... 11 F1
Bull Cl BOZ/IR/WOL NN29 ... 61 G4
Bunting Rd NHTNN/BOU NN2 ... 55 E1
Burford Av NHTNE/MOU NN3 ... 42 D2
Burford Wy WBORO NN8 ... 29 F3
Burleigh Rd NHTNN/BOU NN2 ... 55 E2
Burmans Wy RNHPTN NN7 ... 58 C4
Burnham Cl NHTNS NN4 ... 76 C3
Burns Cl BRIX/LBKBY NN6 ... 46 B3
Burns Rd DAV NN11 ... 34 D5
WBORO NN8 ... 14 D5
Burns St NHTN NN1 ... 55 F3
Burrow's Bush WBORO NN8 ... 16 B3
Burrows Ct NHTNE/MOU NN3 ... 43 E3
Burrows V BRIX/LBKBY NN6 ... 5 E4
Burryport Rd NHTNS NN4 ... 70 B3
Burton Cl DAV NN11 ... 34 D4
Burton Rd IR/RAU/FIN NN9 ... 7 H1
Burtram Cl NHTNE/MOU NN3 ... 57 E1
Burwood Rd NHTNE/MOU NN3 ... 42 B5
Bury Cl RSHD/HF NN10 ... 19 G3
Burystead Pl WBORO NN8 ... 16 A5
Burystead Ri IR/RAU/FIN NN9 ... 11 G1
Burywell Rd WBORO NN8 ... 16 B3
Buscot Park Wy DAV NN11 ... 34 D2
Bush Cl WBORO NN8 ... 15 G4
Bush Hl NHTNE/MOU NN3 ... 42 C5
Bushland Rd NHTNE/MOU NN3 ... 42 C5
Buswell Cl RNHPTN NN7 ... 62 D4
Butcher's La NHTNN/BOU NN2 ... 23 E4
Butlin Cl DAV NN11 ... 50 D1
Butlins La RNHPTN NN7 ... 80 D4
Butterfields WBORO NN8 ... 29 H2
Buttermere WBORO NN8 ... 15 E4
Buttermere Cl
NHTNE/MOU NN3 ... 42 C4
Buttmead RNHPTN NN7 ... 79 F4
Butts Croft Cl NHTNS NN4 ... 76 A2
Butts Hill Crs RNHPTN NN7 ... 65 G4
Butts Rd IR/RAU/FIN NN9 ... 11 G2
NHTNS NN4 ... 76 A2
WBORO NN8 ... 29 G3
Byfield Rd NHTNW NN5 ... 54 C5
By-Pass Wy RNHPTN NN7 ... 73 F5
Byron Crs RSHD/HF NN10 ... 32 C2
Byron Rd WBORO NN8 ... 15 F5
Byron St NHTNN/BOU NN2 ... 55 G1

C

Cabot Cl DAV NN11 ... 35 E4
Calder Gn NHTNW NN5 ... 54 A1
Calstock Cl NHTNE/MOU NN3 ... 56 D3
Calvert Cl WBORO NN8 ... 15 H1
Camberley Cl NHTNE/MOU NN3 ... 43 H5
Camborne Cl NHTNS NN4 ... 68 D4
Cambria Crs NHTNE/MOU NN3 ... 56 C1

e St NHTN NN1 ... 2 B3
/ IR/RAU/FIN NN9 ... 10 B5
IR/RAU/FIN NN9 ... 7 G2
Gn NHTNE/MOU NN3 ... 43 F1
RSHD/HF NN10 ... 19 E4
Ct NHTNE/MOU NN3 ... 57 E2
HTNE/MOU NN3 ... 43 H2
Cl NHTNE/MOU NN3 ... 42 B3
ins NHTNN/BOU NN2 ... 41 F4
I NHTNN/BOU NN2 ... 41 F4
Rd NHTNW NN5 ... 52 D2
Cl IR/RAU/FIN NN9 ... 11 G1
Dr RNHPTN NN7 ... 73 F4
Rd RNHPTN NN7 ... 80 B4
cote BRIX/LBKBY NN6 ... 13 E4
se Cl IR/RAU/FIN NN9 ... 10 B5
RSHD/HF NN10 ... 33 H3
NHTNE/MOU NN3 ... 24 D3
Wy DAV NN11 ... 51 E5
ns IR/RAU/FIN NN9 ... 6 A5
ny NHTNS NN4 ... 75 H2
od Cl
/MOU NN3 ... 44 A4
oe End
BKBY NN6 ... 46 A3
oe Hl
BKBY NN6 ... 46 B4
DAV NN11 ... 51 G3
NHTN NN1 ... 2 D3
Cl NHTNE/MOU NN3 ... 56 D3
Cl RSHD/HF NN10 ... 32 D4
Pk DAV NN11 ... 34 D3
Pl IR/RAU/FIN NN9 ... 9 F3
Rd IR/RAU/FIN NN9 ... 9 F3
Wy DAV NN11 ... 34 C5
NHTN NN1 ... 55 H1
/ NN5 ... 53 E2
HF NN10 ... 33 F3
) NN8 ... 30 A1
Wk NHTNN/BOU NN2 ... 40 C2
y NHTNE/MOU NN3 ... 41 H2
nd Cl BRIX/LBKBY NN6 ... 13 F4
v NHTNE/MOU NN3 ... 42 B4
v DAV NN11 ... 50 D2
d NHTNW NN5 ... 54 B3
) NN8 ... 16 C4
IR/RAU/FIN NN9 ... 11 E2
Wy RSHD/HF NN10 ... 19 E4
Rd NHTNE/MOU NN3 ... 42 C5
t NHTNE/MOU NN3 ... 43 G2
t NHTNE/MOU NN3 ... 57 G1
End BRIX/LBKBY NN6 ... 27 G2
RSHD/HF NN10 ... 19 G4
BOZ/IR/WOL NN29 ... 48 D2
SHD/HF NN10 ... 33 F2
h Dell
/MOU NN3 ... 43 F1
s RNHPTN NN7 ... 62 C4
een Rd RNHPTN NN7 ... 66 A2
HTN NN1 ... 2 E1
) NN8 ... 29 G3
NHTNW NN5 ... 53 G2
WBORO NN8 ... 29 H3
Rd
/MOU NN3 ... 56 D3
NHTNE/MOU NN3 ... 23 H5
t WBORO NN8 ... 29 F1
t NHTNW NN5 ... 54 B4
La NHTNS NN4 ... 76 D5
st NHTN NN1 ... 3 F2
ill La NHTNW NN5 ... 67 H1
d NHTNW NN5 ... 53 H4
ildes NHTNW NN5 ... 39 E5
Crs WBORO NN8 ... 15 G4
La
/WOL NN29 ... 61 G5
NN1 ... 2 E3

E

NHTNS NN4 ... 69 H3
st BRIX/LBKBY NN6 ... 5 E4
on Rd
/WOL NN29 ... 47 E2
BKBY NN6 ... 27 F2
Cl NHTNS NN4 ... 77 E2
TN NN1 ... 3 F2
NHTNE/MOU NN3 ... 43 E1
erfield Ct
/MOU NN3 ... 43 F2
Rd RNHPTN NN7 ... 78 A2
SHD/HF NN10 ... 32 D2
BRIX/LBKBY NN6 ... 5 H1
v North
/BOU NN2 ... 41 F2
v South
/BOU NN2 ... 41 F5
l NHTNN/BOU NN2 ... 41 F4
Wy DAV NN11 ... 51 E2
RNHPTN NN7 ... 79 F4
Cl NHTNW NN5 ... 53 G1
Crs IR/RAU/FIN NN9 ... 8 A1
Rd
/WOL NN29 ... 48 D3
BKBY NN6 ... 4 D5
/FIN NN9 ... 9 F4
NN4 ... 69 E2
/ NN5 ... 53 F2
) NN8 ... 16 B3
SHD/HF NN10 ... 33 F1
Rd IR/RAU/FIN NN9 ... 8 A1
ham Rd
/FIN NN9 ... 11 F1
Ct NHTNE/MOU NN3 ... 24 C5
Ct NHTNE/MOU NN3 ... 57 G1
BOZ/IR/WOL NN29 ... 61 E5
y RNHPTN NN7 ... 60 A3
HTNW NN5 ... 40 B5
ock Ct
/MOU NN3 ... 43 G3
s Ct
/MOU NN3 ... 43 G3
g NHTNS NN4 ... 76 B1
OZ/IR/WOL NN29 ... 31 H4
/FIN NN9 ... 10 C5
NN1 ... 3 K2
NHTNW NN5 ... 53 E1

Ebbw Vale Rd IR/RAU/FIN NN9 ... 18 C1
Ecton Brook Rd
NHTNE/MOU NN3 ... 58 A1
Ecton La BRIX/LBKBY NN6 ... 26 B3
Ecton Park Rd
NHTNE/MOU NN3 ... 44 A4
Ecton St NHTN NN1 ... 3 G3
Eden Cl DAV NN11 ... 50 C3
NHTNE/MOU NN3 ... 42 B3
Edgar Mobbs Wy NHTNW NN5 ... 53 H5
Edgehill Dr DAV NN11 ... 35 E3
Edgehill Rd NHTNW NN5 ... 53 H1
Edgemead Cl NHTNE/MOU NN3 ... 25 E5
Edgemont Rd
NHTNE/MOU NN3 ... 57 E1
Edges Ct NHTNE/MOU NN3 ... 24 C5
Edinburgh Rd
NHTNN/BOU NN2 ... 55 E1
WBORO NN8 ... 29 G3
Edison Cl WBORO NN8 ... 14 C3
Edison Dr NHTNW NN5 ... 67 H1
Edmonds Cl WBORO NN8 ... 30 A2
Edward Cl RSHD/HF NN10 ... 19 G2
Edwardian Cl NHTNS NN4 ... 76 C1
Edward Rd BOZ/IR/WOL NN29 ... 31 H5
Edwards Dr WBORO NN8 ... 15 F4
Edwinstowe Cl
NHTNE/MOU NN3 ... 57 E3
Elder Cl DAV NN11 ... 51 E1
Eldean Rd NHTNW NN5 ... 53 F1
Elderberry Ct
NHTNE/MOU NN3 ... 44 A4
Elder Dr DAV NN11 ... 35 E5
Elgin St NHTNW NN5 ... 54 B4
Elizabeth Cl BRIX/LBKBY NN6 ... 46 A2
WBORO NN8 ... 29 F2
Elizabeth Rd DAV NN11 ... 50 D1
Elizabeth St NHTN NN1 ... 3 J2
Elizabeth Wk NHTN NN1 ... 3 J2
Elizabeth Wy BRIX/LBKBY NN6 ... 45 H2
IR/RAU/FIN NN9 ... 18 C1
RSHD/HF NN10 ... 19 G1
Ellesmere Av NHTNW NN5 ... 53 H3
Ellfield Ct NHTNE/MOU NN3 ... 43 F4
Elliot Wy RSHD/HF NN10 ... 19 E4
Ellison Cl IR/RAU/FIN NN9 ... 11 E1
Elm Cl RNHPTN NN7 ... 72 B3
Elm Gv NHTNS NN4 ... 77 E2
Elmhurst Av NHTNE/MOU NN3 ... 42 A5
Elmhurst Ct NHTNE/MOU NN3 ... 42 A5
Elmington Rd
NHTNE/MOU NN3 ... 44 A1
Elms Dyke DAV NN11 ... 35 G1
Elm St NHTN NN1 ... 2 D1
WBORO NN8 ... 15 H4
Elmwood Wk NHTNW NN5 ... 53 E1
Elsden Rd WBORO NN8 ... 16 C4
Elton Cl NHTNE/MOU NN3 ... 43 H2
Elwes Wy NHTNE/MOU NN3 ... 43 H5
Embankment WBORO NN8 ... 30 C2
Emerald Wy NHTN NN1 ... 2 B4
Emery Cl DAV NN11 ... 35 G1
Emley Cl NHTNE/MOU NN3 ... 57 F1
Emmanuel Cl DAV NN11 ... 51 E4
Enfield Cl NHTNW NN5 ... 52 D2
Ennerdale Cl DAV NN11 ... 50 C2
NHTNE/MOU NN3 ... 42 A4
Ennerdale Rd
NHTNE/MOU NN3 ... 42 A4
RSHD/HF NN10 ... 33 H1
Enstone Ct WBORO NN8 ... 29 F3
Enterprise Rd IR/RAU/FIN NN9 ... 11 F1
Entwood Dr NHTNE/MOU NN3 ... 43 H2
Enyon Cl NHTNE/MOU NN3 ... 24 B3
Epping Wk DAV NN11 ... 34 D5
Epsom Cl RSHD/HF NN10 ... 33 H4
Equestrian Wy RNHPTN NN7 ... 62 D3
Ericsson Cl DAV NN11 ... 35 E4
Ermine Rd NHTNE/MOU NN3 ... 44 A2
Esher Ct NHTNE/MOU NN3 ... 42 D3
Eskdale Av NHTNE/MOU NN3 ... 42 B4
Eskdale Cl WBORO NN8 ... 15 E3
Essex Rd RSHD/HF NN10 ... 33 G3
Essex St NHTNN/BOU NN2 ... 54 D2
Ethel St NHTN NN1 ... 3 H2
Eton Cl RNHPTN NN7 ... 63 E3
Euston Rd NHTNS NN4 ... 69 E2
Evans Cl DAV NN11 ... 51 G3
Evelyn Wy BOZ/IR/WOL NN29 ... 32 A5
Evenley Rd NHTNN/BOU NN2 ... 41 E2
Evensford Wk IR/RAU/FIN NN9 ... 18 B1
Everdon Cl NHTNN/BOU NN2 ... 41 G3
Everdon Pk DAV NN11 ... 34 C4
Everitt Cl WBORO NN8 ... 30 B2
Evesham Cl WBORO NN8 ... 29 G3
Evesham Ct NHTNE/MOU NN3 ... 25 G5
Ewenfield Rd IR/RAU/FIN NN9 ... 7 H2
Excalibur Cl NHTNW NN5 ... 53 E3
Excelsior Gdns NHTNW NN5 ... 52 D2
Exeter Cl DAV NN11 ... 51 E4
Exeter Pl NHTN NN1 ... 3 G1
Exmoor Cl NHTNE/MOU NN3 ... 56 D3
Express Cl IR/RAU/FIN NN9 ... 18 C1

F

Fairfield RNHPTN NN7 ... 78 D1
Fairfield Rd NHTNN/BOU NN2 ... 41 H5
Fairground Wy
NHTNE/MOU NN3 ... 57 E3
Fairhurst Wy BRIX/LBKBY NN6 ... 46 B3
Fairmead Crs RSHD/HF NN10 ... 32 D4
Fairmead Ri NHTNN/BOU NN2 ... 40 B1
Fair Mile NHTNN/BOU NN2 ... 40 C1
Fairoaks Dr IR/RAU/FIN NN9 ... 11 E1
The Fairoaks NHTNE/MOU NN3 ... 57 F2
Fairway NHTNN/BOU NN2 ... 41 G5
The Fairway DAV NN11 ... 51 G2
IR/RAU/FIN NN9 ... 6 A5
Falconers Ri NHTNS NN4 ... 68 C5
Falcutt Wy NHTNN/BOU NN2 ... 41 F1
Fallowfield IR/RAU/FIN NN9 ... 15 G1
Fallow Wk NHTNN/BOU NN2 ... 40 C1
Faracre Ct NHTNE/MOU NN3 ... 57 H1
Faraday Cl DAV NN11 ... 34 C5
NHTNW NN5 ... 53 H5

WBORO NN8 ... 14 C3
Faramir Pl NHTNE/MOU NN3 ... 43 H1
Far Brook BRIX/LBKBY NN6 ... 12 D1
Far End NHTNW NN5 ... 54 B4
Faringdon Ct NHTNE/MOU NN3 ... 25 G5
Farmbrook Ct
NHTNE/MOU NN3 ... 43 F2
Farm Cl NHTNN/BOU NN2 ... 40 D3
Farmclose Rd NHTNS NN4 ... 76 C2
Far Meadow Ct
NHTNE/MOU NN3 ... 43 E2
Farmers Cl NHTNS NN4 ... 76 C3
Farm Field Ct
NHTNE/MOU NN3 ... 43 E2
Farmhill Rd NHTNE/MOU NN3 ... 43 G1
Farm Rd WBORO NN8 ... 15 G1
Farnborough Dr DAV NN11 ... 34 D3
Farndish Cl RSHD/HF NN10 ... 32 C2
Farndish Rd BOZ/IR/WOL NN29 ... 31 H5
Farndon Cl NHTNE/MOU NN3 ... 43 G1
Farnham Dr RSHD/HF NN10 ... 32 D4
Farnworth Cl NHTNW NN5 ... 53 G1
Farraxton Sq NHTNS NN4 ... 68 A3
Favell Wy NHTNE/MOU NN3 ... 56 D2
Fawsley Rd NHTNS NN4 ... 69 E3
Faxton Cl NHTNN/BOU NN2 ... 41 F3
Fellmead Rd NHTNE/MOU NN3 ... 44 A2
Fellows Cl BOZ/IR/WOL NN29 ... 48 C2
Fell Wk WBORO NN8 ... 15 F3
Fengate Cl NHTNE/MOU NN3 ... 44 A2
Fennel Ct NHTNS NN4 ... 76 B3
Fenners Cl RSHD/HF NN10 ... 33 H2
Ferndale Rd NHTNE/MOU NN3 ... 42 D5
Fernie Fld NHTNE/MOU NN3 ... 42 C1
Fernie Wy WBORO NN8 ... 29 F1
Fernmoor Dr IR/RAU/FIN NN9 ... 9 F4
Fern Rd RSHD/HF NN10 ... 32 C1
Ferrestone Rd WBORO NN8 ... 16 A3
Ferris Rw NHTNE/MOU NN3 ... 57 F3
Ferro Flds BRIX/LBKBY NN6 ... 5 E3
Festival Cl IR/RAU/FIN NN9 ... 9 H1
Fetter St NHTN NN1 ... 2 E4
Fettledine Rd IR/RAU/FIN NN9 ... 9 H1
Fieldgate Cl NHTNS NN4 ... 76 D3
Fieldmill Rd NHTNE/MOU NN3 ... 57 H1
Field Rose Sq
NHTNE/MOU NN3 ... 44 A5
Fields Vw WBORO NN8 ... 16 B5
Fieldway NHTNE/MOU NN3 ... 56 B1
Fienesgate NHTNS NN4 ... 67 H4
Fiennes Ct DAV NN11 ... 34 D3
Fife St NHTNW NN5 ... 54 B3
Filleigh Wy NHTNE/MOU NN3 ... 56 C3
Finedon Rd IR/RAU/FIN NN9 ... 8 C3
WBORO NN8 ... 16 B3
Finney Dr NHTNS NN4 ... 76 C5
Firbank Cl NHTNE/MOU NN3 ... 57 F2
Firdale Av RSHD/HF NN10 ... 19 F5
First Av WBORO NN8 ... 29 F2
The Firs DAV NN11 ... 51 E1
First La NHTNW NN5 ... 54 B4
Firsview Dr NHTNW NN5 ... 53 F1
Fir Tree Gv BOZ/IR/WOL NN29 ... 61 G5
Fir Tree Wk NHTNE/MOU NN3 ... 43 E5
Fishers Cl NHTNE/MOU NN3 ... 57 H1
Fishpond Cl RNHPTN NN7 ... 73 F4
Fishponds Rd
NHTNE/MOU NN3 ... 43 G5
Fish St NHTN NN1 ... 2 E3
Fitzroy Pl NHTN NN1 ... 2 B3
Fitzwilliam Leys
RSHD/HF NN10 ... 19 F2
Fitzwilliam Rd IR/RAU/FIN NN9 ... 9 F3
Fitzwilliam St RSHD/HF NN10 ... 33 E2
Five Acres Fold NHTNS NN4 ... 68 B2
Flaxlands Ct NHTNE/MOU NN3 ... 43 F4
Flaxwell Ct NHTNE/MOU NN3 ... 57 F2
Fleetwind Dr NHTNS NN4 ... 76 B1
Fleming Cl WBORO NN8 ... 14 D2
Fletcher Rd RSHD/HF NN10 ... 33 E1
Flintcomb Ri NHTNE/MOU NN3 ... 43 H4
Flinters Cl NHTNS NN4 ... 76 D2
Flore Hl RNHPTN NN7 ... 63 F2
Florence Rd NHTN NN1 ... 3 K1
Floribunda Dr NHTNS NN4 ... 68 B2
Flowerhill Dr WBORO NN8 ... 16 B3
Flying Dutchman Wy
DAV NN11 ... 50 C1
Folly La RNHPTN NN7 ... 36 B5
Forest Ct RSHD/HF NN10 ... 33 H1
Forest Rd NHTNS NN4 ... 69 E2
Forfar St NHTNW NN5 ... 54 B3
Fort Pl NHTN NN1 ... 2 B3
Fosberry Cl NHTNS NN4 ... 76 D2
Foskett Cl RSHD/HF NN10 ... 33 E1
Foskitt Ct NHTNE/MOU NN3 ... 57 H2
Fosse Cl WBORO NN8 ... 29 F3
Fosse Gn RSHD/HF NN10 ... 33 G1
Foundry Pl DAV NN11 ... 51 E3
Foundry St NHTN NN1 ... 2 D5
Fourth Av WBORO NN8 ... 29 F1
Fowey Cl WBORO NN8 ... 15 E3
Fox Covert Dr RNHPTN NN7 ... 81 E5
Foxcovert Rd
NHTNE/MOU NN3 ... 43 H2
Foxendale Sq
NHTNE/MOU NN3 ... 44 B5
Foxford Cl NHTNS NN4 ... 68 B5
Foxglove Cl RSHD/HF NN10 ... 33 G4
Foxgrove Av NHTNN/BOU NN2 ... 40 C3
Fox Hill Rd NHTNE/MOU NN3 ... 44 B5
Foxwell Sq NHTNE/MOU NN3 ... 43 F1
Foxwood Cl RSHD/HF NN10 ... 32 C2
Franciscan Cl RSHD/HF NN10 ... 32 D4
Francis Ct RSHD/HF NN10 ... 18 C5
Francis Dickins Cl
BOZ/IR/WOL NN29 ... 49 E2
Francis St IR/RAU/FIN NN9 ... 10 D4
NHTN NN1 ... 2 C1
Franklin Crs NHTNW NN5 ... 53 H3
Franklin's Cl BRIX/LBKBY NN6 ... 44 D3
Franklin St NHTNW NN5 ... 54 B4
Franklin Wy DAV NN11 ... 35 E4
Fraser Cl DAV NN11 ... 51 F2
Fraser Rd NHTNE/MOU NN3 ... 42 D2
Freehold St NHTNN/BOU NN2 ... 55 E2
Freeman Wy IR/RAU/FIN NN9 ... 8 B1
Freeschool St NHTN NN1 ... 2 C4
Frencham Cl NHTNS NN4 ... 68 B2
Friar's Av NHTNS NN4 ... 68 D4

Friar's Cl NHTNS NN4 ... 68 D4
Friars Cl WBORO NN8 ... 30 A1
Friar's Crs NHTNS NN4 ... 69 E4
Friary Cl DAV NN11 ... 51 F2
Frinton Cl RSHD/HF NN10 ... 32 D4
Frobisher Cl DAV NN11 ... 51 G2
Frog Hall BRIX/LBKBY NN6 ... 4 C4
Frost Ct BOZ/IR/WOL NN29 ... 47 F1
Frosts Ct NHTNS NN4 ... 76 C3
Frosty Hollow NHTNS NN4 ... 76 A2
Froxhill Crs BRIX/LBKBY NN6 ... 4 C5
Fuchsia Cl NHTNE/MOU NN3 ... 56 C4
Fuchsia Wy RSHD/HF NN10 ... 33 F5
Fulford Dr NHTNN/BOU NN2 ... 41 G4
Fulleburn Ct NHTNE/MOU NN3 ... 43 E4
Fuller Rd NHTNE/MOU NN3 ... 24 C4
Fullingdale Rd
NHTNE/MOU NN3 ... 42 B5
Fullwell Rd BOZ/IR/WOL NN29 ... 61 G3
Fulmar La WBORO NN8 ... 16 A1
Furber Ct NHTNE/MOU NN3 ... 42 D3
Furnace Dr DAV NN11 ... 34 C5
Furnace La IR/RAU/FIN NN9 ... 6 B1
RNHPTN NN7 ... 64 B3
Furnells Cl IR/RAU/FIN NN9 ... 11 F1
Furze Rd RNHPTN NN7 ... 72 B3
Furze Wk NHTNN/BOU NN2 ... 41 G5
Fusilier Rd DAV NN11 ... 50 D3
Fusilier Wy RNHPTN NN7 ... 62 C3
Fylingdale NHTNN/BOU NN2 ... 40 B2

G

Gable Cl DAV NN11 ... 50 D3
Gable Court Ms
NHTNE/MOU NN3 ... 56 D1
Gadesby Ct NHTNE/MOU NN3 ... 43 E4
Gainsborough Dr WBORO NN8 ... 15 H2
Galahad Ct NHTNW NN5 ... 53 E3
Galane Cl NHTNS NN4 ... 67 H4
Gallery Cl NHTNE/MOU NN3 ... 43 G1
Gallfield Ct NHTNE/MOU NN3 ... 57 H2
Gallowhill Rd NHTNS NN4 ... 70 B4
Gambrel Rd NHTNW NN5 ... 53 H4
Gannet La WBORO NN8 ... 16 A1
Ganton Cl DAV NN11 ... 51 G2
The Gap BOZ/IR/WOL NN29 ... 49 E3
Gardenfield RSHD/HF NN10 ... 19 F4
Gardenfields Cl IR/RAU/FIN NN9 ... 9 H1
Gardner Cl IR/RAU/FIN NN9 ... 11 E1
Garfield Cl NHTNN/BOU NN2 ... 41 E4
Garfield St NHTNN/BOU NN2 ... 40 D4
Garners Wy RNHPTN NN7 ... 52 A3
Garrick Rd NHTN NN1 ... 56 B3
Garrow Cl IR/RAU/FIN NN9 ... 9 E3
Garsdale NHTNN/BOU NN2 ... 40 B1
Gatelodge Cl NHTNE/MOU NN3 ... 43 E1
Gateway Cl NHTNS NN4 ... 76 D2
Gawaine Ct NHTNW NN5 ... 53 E3
Gayhurst Cl NHTNE/MOU NN3 ... 24 B5
Gayton Rd RNHPTN NN7 ... 78 D3
Gedling Cl NHTNE/MOU NN3 ... 57 F2
Geldock Rd NHTNE/MOU NN3 ... 57 G1
Gentian Cl RSHD/HF NN10 ... 33 F4
George Nutt Ct NHTNS NN4 ... 69 E3
George Rw NHTN NN1 ... 2 D4
Georges Av RNHPTN NN7 ... 65 G5
Georges Cl RNHPTN NN7 ... 65 G5
George St IR/RAU/FIN NN9 ... 9 E5
RSHD/HF NN10 ... 33 F2
WBORO NN8 ... 16 A4
Gervase Sq NHTNE/MOU NN3 ... 58 A1
Gibbsacre Ct NHTNE/MOU NN3 ... 58 A1
Gibson La NHTNW NN5 ... 54 B2
Gilbey Cl IR/RAU/FIN NN9 ... 6 A5
Gillitts Rd WBORO NN8 ... 29 G1
Gillsway NHTNN/BOU NN2 ... 40 C3
Gipsy La BOZ/IR/WOL NN29 ... 30 D4
Gisburne Rd WBORO NN8 ... 16 A3
Glade Cl NHTNE/MOU NN3 ... 57 H1
The Glade IR/RAU/FIN NN9 ... 6 A5
Gladiator Cl NHTNS NN4 ... 76 D3
Gladstone Cl NHTNW NN5 ... 54 C2
Gladstone Rd NHTNW NN5 ... 54 C1
Glaisedale Cl NHTNN/BOU NN2 ... 40 B2
Glamis Cl RSHD/HF NN10 ... 33 H3
Glasgow St NHTNW NN5 ... 54 B3
Glassbrook Rd RSHD/HF NN10 ... 32 D2
Glastonbury Rd NHTNS NN4 ... 69 E4
Glebe Av NHTNS NN4 ... 69 G5
Glebe Cl NHTNS NN4 ... 69 G5
Glebe Farm Cl NHTNS NN4 ... 76 A4
Glebe Farm Ct
BOZ/IR/WOL NN29 ... 47 F1
Glebeland Crs NHTNW NN5 ... 54 C2
Glebeland Gdns NHTNW NN5 ... 54 B1
Glebeland Rd NHTNW NN5 ... 54 B1
Glebeland Wk NHTNW NN5 ... 54 B2
Glebe La BRIX/LBKBY NN6 ... 13 E4
NHTNS NN4 ... 71 E3
RNHPTN NN7 ... 20 C5
Glebe Rd BRIX/LBKBY NN6 ... 27 E1
RNHPTN NN7 ... 58 C4
The Glebe DAV NN11 ... 51 E4
Glebe Wy NHTNS NN4 ... 69 G5
RNHPTN NN7 ... 58 C4
Glen Av RNHPTN NN7 ... 78 D1
Glen Bank WBORO NN8 ... 16 A5
Glendale Ct NHTNE/MOU NN3 ... 58 A1
Gleneagles Cl DAV NN11 ... 51 G2
Gleneagles Dr WBORO NN8 ... 15 F2
Glenfield Cl RSHD/HF NN10 ... 32 D1
Glenfield Dr BOZ/IR/WOL NN29 ... 47 F2
Glengary NHTNE/MOU NN3 ... 24 D5
Glenville NHTNE/MOU NN3 ... 42 B3
Gloucester Av NHTNS NN4 ... 68 D3
Gloucester Cl NHTNS NN4 ... 68 D3
RNHPTN NN7 ... 62 D3
Gloucester Crs NHTNS NN4 ... 68 D3
RSHD/HF NN10 ... 33 G1
Glovers Cl IR/RAU/FIN NN9 ... 18 C1
Glovers La IR/RAU/FIN NN9 ... 11 E3
Godwin Wk NHTNW NN5 ... 39 H5
Goldcrest Ct NHTNE/MOU NN3 ... 43 G2
Goldenash Ct
NHTNE/MOU NN3 ... 43 F3
Golding Cl DAV NN11 ... 51 E2

Goldings Rd NHTNE/MOU NN3 ... 43 G2
Goldsmith Rd WBORO NN8 ... 15 E5
Gold St NHTN NN1 ... 2 C4
WBORO NN8 ... 16 A4
Golf La BRIX/LBKBY NN6 ... 21 G4
Goodens La BOZ/IR/WOL NN29 ... 47 H1
Goodwin Cl WBORO NN8 ... 15 H1
Goodwood Av
NHTNE/MOU NN3 ... 41 H3
Goodwood Rd RSHD/HF NN10 ... 33 H4
Gordon Rd WBORO NN8 ... 16 B4
Gordon St NHTNN/BOU NN2 ... 54 D2
RSHD/HF NN10 ... 32 D2
Gorse Cl NHTNN/BOU NN2 ... 40 D2
Goulsbra Rd RSHD/HF NN10 ... 33 H4
Gowerton Rd NHTNS NN4 ... 70 A4
Grafton Cl WBORO NN8 ... 15 F2
Grafton Pl NHTN NN1 ... 2 C1
Grafton Rd RNHPTN NN7 ... 80 C4
RSHD/HF NN10 ... 33 H2
Grafton St NHTN NN1 ... 2 C1
Grafton Vw NHTNS NN4 ... 76 C2
Grafton Wy NHTNW NN5 ... 39 F5
RNHPTN NN7 ... 74 A1
Granary Ct NHTNS NN4 ... 76 A1
Granary Rd NHTNS NN4 ... 76 A1
Grandborough Cl
BRIX/LBKBY NN6 ... 5 E5
Grand Union Canal Wk
DAV NN11 ... 34 A1
NHTNS NN4 ... 2 B7
RNHPTN NN7 ... 74 C3
Grand Union Canal Walk
& Nene Wy NHTN NN1 ... 2 C6
Grange Av NHTNW NN5 ... 53 F2
Grange Cl BOZ/IR/WOL NN29 ... 31 H5
BRIX/LBKBY NN6 ... 46 A2
RNHPTN NN7 ... 73 E4
Grange Ct BRIX/LBKBY NN6 ... 4 D4
Grange La BRIX/LBKBY NN6 ... 13 F4
Grange Rd IR/RAU/FIN NN9 ... 6 A5
IR/RAU/FIN NN9 ... 10 B5
NHTNE/MOU NN3 ... 42 C4
Grangeway RSHD/HF NN10 ... 33 E4
Grangewood NHTNS NN4 ... 75 G1
Grant Rd WBORO NN8 ... 16 B4
Grasmere Wy RSHD/HF NN10 ... 19 F1
Graspin La NHTNE/MOU NN3 ... 56 D2
Grasscroft NHTNN/BOU NN2 ... 40 C3
Grassmere Av
NHTNE/MOU NN3 ... 43 E5
Grass Slade BRIX/LBKBY NN6 ... 5 E4
Gravely St RSHD/HF NN10 ... 32 D2
Gray Cl BRIX/LBKBY NN6 ... 46 C3
Gray St BOZ/IR/WOL NN29 ... 31 G5
NHTN NN1 ... 55 G3
Great Billing Wy
NHTNE/MOU NN3 ... 44 A2
Great Cl BRIX/LBKBY NN6 ... 21 H3
Great Field Ct
NHTNE/MOU NN3 ... 43 E2
Great Gull Crs
NHTNE/MOU NN3 ... 43 G1
Great Holme Ct
NHTNE/MOU NN3 ... 43 E2
Great La RNHPTN NN7 ... 65 F5
Greatmeadow Rd
NHTNE/MOU NN3 ... 43 H3
Great Park St WBORO NN8 ... 16 A4
Great Russell St NHTN NN1 ... 3 F1
Greenacre Dr RSHD/HF NN10 ... 33 F5
Greenaway Cl RNHPTN NN7 ... 79 G4
Green Cl IR/RAU/FIN NN9 ... 8 D5
WBORO NN8 ... 15 E2
Green Dale Sq
NHTNE/MOU NN3 ... 44 A5
Green End NHTNN/BOU NN2 ... 40 D5
Greenfield Av
NHTNE/MOU NN3 ... 42 A4
Greenfield Rd
NHTNE/MOU NN3 ... 42 A4
Greenfield Wy RSHD/HF NN10 ... 33 E3
Greenfinch Dr
NHTNE/MOU NN3 ... 42 C1
Greenglades NHTNS NN4 ... 67 H4
Greenhill Crs DAV NN11 ... 50 D1
Greenhills Cl NHTNN/BOU NN2 ... 40 D1
Greenhills Rd
NHTNN/BOU NN2 ... 40 D1
Green La IR/RAU/FIN NN9 ... 10 B5
NHTNS NN4 ... 76 C3
Green Rd RNHPTN NN7 ... 72 C3
Greenside RNHPTN NN7 ... 79 F4
Green St BOZ/IR/WOL NN29 ... 49 E3
NHTN NN1 ... 2 B4
RNHPTN NN7 ... 75 E4
The Green NHTN NN1 ... 2 C4
NHTNN/BOU NN2 ... 40 D4
NHTNS NN4 ... 69 H5
RNHPTN NN7 ... 63 H2
Greenview Dr
NHTNN/BOU NN2 ... 41 G5
Greenway NHTNE/MOU NN3 ... 56 C1
Greenway Av
NHTNE/MOU NN3 ... 42 D3
The Greenway DAV NN11 ... 51 E4
Greenwood Cl
NHTNE/MOU NN3 ... 24 C4
Greenwood Rd NHTNW NN5 ... 54 C4
Greeves Cl NHTNW NN5 ... 52 D1
Gregory St NHTN NN1 ... 2 C4
Grenadier Rd DAV NN11 ... 50 C3
Grendon Wk NHTNE/MOU NN3 ... 41 H3
Grenville Cl DAV NN11 ... 51 G3
Gresham Dr NHTNS NN4 ... 67 H3
Gresley Cl DAV NN11 ... 34 C5
Gretton Ct WBORO NN8 ... 15 F2
Greville Av NHTNE/MOU NN3 ... 42 A3
Greville Cl NHTNN/BOU NN2 ... 23 E4
Greyfriars NHTN NN1 ... 2 D3
Greyfriars Rd DAV NN11 ... 50 D4
The Greys RNHPTN NN7 ... 62 D3
Griffiths Cl NHTNW NN5 ... 52 D2
Griffith St RSHD/HF NN10 ... 33 F3
Grimmer Wk IR/RAU/FIN NN9 ... 18 B1
Grombold Av IR/RAU/FIN NN9 ... 11 E2
Grosvenor Gdns
NHTNN/BOU NN2 ... 41 F3
Groundwell Ct
NHTNE/MOU NN3 ... 57 F1

Grovebury Dell
NHTNN/BOU NN2 40 C3
Grove Farm La
NHTNE/MOU NN3 24 C2
Grovelands DAV NN11 50 C3
Grove Pl IR/RAU/FIN NN9 11 F3
Grove Rd NHTN NN1 3 G1
RNHPTN NN7 72 B2
RSHD/HF NN10 33 G2
Grove St IR/RAU/FIN NN9 11 E3
RSHD/HF NN10 19 G3
WBORO NN8 15 G5
The Grove BOZ/IR/WOL NN29 48 D4
NHTNE/MOU NN3 24 C2
RNHPTN NN7 81 E5
Grove Wy IR/RAU/FIN NN9 7 G3
Guildhall Rd NHTN NN1 2 E4
Guillemot La WBORO NN8 16 A2
Gurston Ri NHTNE/MOU NN3 44 A3

H

Hachenburg Pl RSHD/HF NN10 19 G4
Hackwood Rd DAV NN11 51 G4
Haddon Cl RSHD/HF NN10 33 E4
WBORO NN8 15 F1
Haines Rd NHTNS NN4 69 E2
Halford Wy DAV NN11 35 G1
Hallam Cl NHTNE/MOU NN3 24 B5
Hall Av RSHD/HF NN10 33 E3
Hall Cl NHTNW NN5 53 G4
RNHPTN NN7 66 B1
Hall Dr IR/RAU/FIN NN9 7 G2
Hall Farm Cl BRIX/LBKBY NN6 4 D3
Hall La RNHPTN NN7 36 C5
Hall Piece Cl NHTNE/MOU NN3 44 A4
Halswell Ct NHTNE/MOU NN3 42 D3
Hambledon Ri NHTNS NN4 68 A2
Hamilton La RNHPTN NN7 36 D3
Hamlet Gn NHTNW NN5 54 B2
Ham Meadow Dr
NHTNE/MOU NN3 44 A5
Hammerstone La NHTNS NN4 68 B2
Hampton St NHTN NN1 54 D3
Hamsterly Pk
NHTNE/MOU NN3 43 G1
Hanbury Cl DAV NN11 34 D3
Handcross Wy RSHD/HF NN10 19 G5
Handley Cl NHTNW NN5 53 E1
Hanemill Ct NHTNE/MOU NN3 58 A1
Hangerfield Ct
NHTNE/MOU NN3 43 F3
Hanover Ct NHTNE/MOU NN3 43 H3
Harborough Rd
BRIX/LBKBY NN6 4 D4
NHTNN/BOU NN2 41 E2
RSHD/HF NN10 33 G3
Harborough Rd North
NHTNN/BOU NN2 22 D5
Harborough Wy
RSHD/HF NN10 33 G3
Harcourt St IR/RAU/FIN NN9 11 F2
Harcourt Wy NHTNS NN4 68 A2
Hardingstone La NHTNS NN4 69 F5
Harding Ter NHTN NN1 2 C1
Hardlands Rd NHTNW NN5 53 G2
Hardwater Rd
BOZ/IR/WOL NN29 47 E3
Hardwick Cl WBORO NN8 15 G4
Hardwick Hall Wy DAV NN11 34 D2
Hardwick Rd IR/RAU/FIN NN9 14 B1
NHTNS NN4 69 E5
WBORO NN8 15 E3
Hardy Dr NHTNS NN4 76 D1
Harebell Sq NHTNE/MOU NN3 44 B5
Harefield Rd NHTNE/MOU NN3 43 H2
Harefoot Cl NHTNW NN5 53 F2
Harksome Hl NHTNS NN4 68 A3
Harlestone Rd
BRIX/LBKBY NN6 21 G3
NHTNW NN5 53 H1
RNHPTN NN7 38 D2
Harmans Wy RNHPTN NN7 62 D3
Harold St NHTN NN1 3 G3
Harrier Pk NHTNS NN4 68 D5
Harris Cl IR/RAU/FIN NN9 11 F1
NHTNS NN4 76 D1
Harrison Cl WBORO NN8 15 F4
Harrison Ct RNHPTN NN7 65 F5
Harrold Rd BOZ/IR/WOL NN29 61 G4
Harrowden Rd IR/RAU/FIN NN9 7 G3
NHTNS NN4 70 B3
WBORO NN8 15 G2
Harrowick La BRIX/LBKBY NN6 46 A3
Harrow Wy NHTNN/BOU NN2 40 B1
Hartburn Cl NHTNE/MOU NN3 58 A2
Hartwell Cl NHTNN/BOU NN2 41 F2
Hartwell Rd RNHPTN NN7 81 E4
Harvest Cl DAV NN11 35 F3
Harvest Wy NHTNN/BOU NN2 40 B2
Harvey Cl IR/RAU/FIN NN9 10 D3
Harvey La NHTNE/MOU NN3 24 B4
Harvey Reeves Rd NHTNW NN5 54 C5
Harvey Rd RSHD/HF NN10 33 F5
WBORO NN8 29 G1
Haselrig Sq NHTNS NN4 68 B3
Hassocks Hedge NHTNS NN4 67 G3
Hastings Rd NHTNN/BOU NN2 41 F3
Hatfield Cl WBORO NN8 15 E2
Hatton Av WBORO NN8 15 H4
Hatton Cl NHTNE/MOU NN3 42 A1
Hatton Park Rd WBORO NN8 15 G4
Hatton St WBORO NN8 15 G3
Havelock St WBORO NN8 16 A4
Haven Cl NHTNW NN5 54 C3
Hawke Rd DAV NN11 51 G3
Hawk Esbeard Pl
NHTNE/MOU NN3 44 A5
Hawkins Cl DAV NN11 51 G1
Hawk Rdg NHTNS NN4 68 B4
Hawksmoor Wy NHTNW NN5 53 H1
Hawksnest NHTNS NN4 68 C5
Hawkstone Cl NHTNW NN5 53 H4
Hawthorn Dr DAV NN11 35 E5
Hawthorne Rd IR/RAU/FIN NN9 8 A2
Hawthorn Rd
NHTNE/MOU NN3 56 A1
The Hawthorns RSHD/HF NN10 19 F3
Hawthorn Wy WBORO NN8 15 G5
Hay Cl RSHD/HF NN10 33 F4
Haycroft Wk NHTNN/BOU NN2 40 C2
Hayden Av IR/RAU/FIN NN9 8 A1
Hayden Rd RSHD/HF NN10 33 G2
Haydown Gn NHTNW NN5 53 H2
Hayeswood Rd
NHTNE/MOU NN3 43 F3
Hay La IR/RAU/FIN NN9 9 F5
The Hayride NHTNS NN4 75 G1
The Haystack DAV NN11 35 F3
Hayway IR/RAU/FIN NN9 9 E5
RSHD/HF NN10 19 E5
Hazelden Cl BOZ/IR/WOL NN29 48 D4
Hazeldene Rd
NHTNN/BOU NN2 41 H5
Hazelwood Rd NHTN NN1 3 F4
Headingley Rd RSHD/HF NN10 33 H2
The Headlands
NHTNE/MOU NN3 42 C5
WBORO NN8 15 H3
Healey Cl NHTNE/MOU NN3 44 B3
Heatherbreea Gdns
RSHD/HF NN10 32 C1
Heatherdale Wy
NHTNN/BOU NN2 41 G4
Heather La NHTNE/MOU NN3 43 E3
The Heathers
BOZ/IR/WOL NN29 49 E3
Heathfield Wy NHTNW NN5 40 C5
Heath Ri WBORO NN8 15 F3
Heathville NHTNW NN5 54 B1
H E Bates Wy RSHD/HF NN10 32 D2
Hecham Wy RSHD/HF NN10 19 F2
Hedge End NHTNS NN4 76 A2
Hedgely Ct NHTNS NN4 68 C3
Hedgerow Dr
NHTNN/BOU NN2 * 40 C2
Hedgerow Wy DAV NN11 35 E3
The Hedges RSHD/HF NN10 19 G5
Hedgeway NHTNS NN4 76 A2
Hellidon Cl NHTNN/BOU NN2 41 F3
Helmdon Crs NHTNN/BOU NN2 41 E2
Helmdon Rd NHTNN/BOU NN2 41 E2
Hemans Rd DAV NN11 34 D5
Hembury Pl NHTNS NN4 68 B2
Hemmingwell Rd WBORO NN8 16 A2
Henley Cl WBORO NN8 15 E2
Henry Bird Ct NHTNS NN4 2 E6
Henry St NHTN NN1 55 G3
Henshaw Rd WBORO NN8 29 G1
Hensmans La
BOZ/IR/WOL NN29 61 F4
Herbert St NHTN NN1 2 C2
Hereward Rd NHTNS NN4 68 D3
Heritage Wy IR/RAU/FIN NN9 11 G1
Hermitage Wy NHTNS NN4 76 B1
Herne Hill Ct NHTNS NN4 68 A3
Heron Cl WBORO NN8 16 A2
Heronsford NHTNS NN4 68 A5
Herriotts La WBORO NN8 16 A4
Hertford Ct DAV NN11 51 E5
NHTNE/MOU NN3 57 G1
Hervey Cl NHTNE/MOU NN3 42 D5
Hervey St NHTN NN1 3 F1
Hester St NHTNN/BOU NN2 55 E2
Hever Cl RSHD/HF NN10 33 G4
Hewlett's Cl BOZ/IR/WOL NN29 61 G5
Hexham Ct NHTNS NN4 68 C3
Hibiscus Cl NHTNE/MOU NN3 56 C4
Hickmire BOZ/IR/WOL NN29 48 D2
Hidcote Cl NHTNS NN4 76 A1
WBORO NN8 29 F3
Hidcote Wy DAV NN11 34 D2
Higgins Sq NHTNS NN4 68 B3
Higham Rd BOZ/IR/WOL NN29 31 E3
RSHD/HF NN10 19 F5
Highdown Cl NHTNS NN4 68 A2
Highfield Rd BRIX/LBKBY NN6 27 G1
DAV NN11 50 D1
IR/RAU/FIN NN9 9 F4
NHTN NN1 56 A1
RSHD/HF NN10 32 D3
WBORO NN8 16 B4
Highfield St IR/RAU/FIN NN9 8 A1
High Greeve NHTNS NN4 77 E2
Highgrove Ct RSHD/HF NN10 33 F2
Highlands Av NHTNE/MOU NN3 41 H3
Highlands Dr DAV NN11 34 D4
High March DAV NN11 51 G4
High March Cl DAV NN11 51 G4
High Slade BRIX/LBKBY NN6 13 E1
High St BOZ/IR/WOL NN29 31 H4
BOZ/IR/WOL NN29 47 G1
BOZ/IR/WOL NN29 48 D3
BOZ/IR/WOL NN29 61 G5
BRIX/LBKBY NN6 4 D3
BRIX/LBKBY NN6 13 E5
BRIX/LBKBY NN6 44 D3
BRIX/LBKBY NN6 46 A3
DAV NN11 51 E3
IR/RAU/FIN NN9 7 H1
IR/RAU/FIN NN9 9 E5
IR/RAU/FIN NN9 11 F1
NHTNE/MOU NN3 24 C3
NHTNE/MOU NN3 44 A5
NHTNE/MOU NN3 56 D1
NHTNN/BOU NN2 40 D4
NHTNS NN4 71 E2
NHTNS NN4 76 A5
RNHPTN NN7 52 A4
RNHPTN NN7 62 D3
RNHPTN NN7 63 H2
RNHPTN NN7 65 F5
RNHPTN NN7 75 E4
RNHPTN NN7 78 A1
RNHPTN NN7 79 F4
RNHPTN NN7 80 D4
RSHD/HF NN10 33 F2
WBORO NN8 15 H4
High St South RSHD/HF NN10 33 F3
High Vw NHTNS NN4 76 C2
High Woods BRIX/LBKBY NN6 26 B4
Hillary Cl DAV NN11 34 D4
Hillary Rd RSHD/HF NN10 32 D3
Hillberry Ri NHTNE/MOU NN3 44 B3
Hill Cl NHTNW NN5 39 G5
Hill Crest RNHPTN NN7 79 E2
Hillcrest Av NHTNE/MOU NN3 42 A4
Hillcrest Rd RNHPTN NN7 78 A2
Hilldrop Rd NHTNS NN4 75 G1
Hill Farm Ri NHTNS NN4 68 B5
Hill House Gdns
IR/RAU/FIN NN9 10 B5
Hillside DAV NN11 51 G2
Hillside Cl BOZ/IR/WOL NN29 61 G5
Hillside Crs RNHPTN NN7 64 C3
Hillside Rd RNHPTN NN7 63 F1
WBORO NN8 16 C2
Hillside Wy NHTNE/MOU NN3 56 C2
Hill St IR/RAU/FIN NN9 11 F2
WBORO NN8 15 H5
The Hill NHTNS NN4 71 E3
Hilltop RNHPTN NN7 79 E2
Hilltop Cl BRIX/LBKBY NN6 4 D5
Hind Stile RSHD/HF NN10 19 F4
Hinton Cl NHTNN/BOU NN2 41 E2
Hinton Rd NHTNN/BOU NN2 41 E2
Hinwick Rd BOZ/IR/WOL NN29 48 D3
Hirondelle Cl NHTNW NN5 52 D1
Hobby Cl NHTNS NN4 68 D5
Hocknell Cl NHTNS NN4 76 D2
Hodges La RNHPTN NN7 66 B1
Hodnet Cl NHTNS NN4 76 A1
Hoe Wy RNHPTN NN7 80 C4
Hogarth Cl WBORO NN8 15 H2
Holbein Gdns NHTNS NN4 68 A5
Holbush Wy IR/RAU/FIN NN9 9 E3
Holcot Cl WBORO NN8 15 G1
Holcot Rd BRIX/LBKBY NN6 4 D4
NHTNE/MOU NN3 24 C1
Holcutt Cl NHTNS NN4 76 D1
Holdenby Rd NHTNN/BOU NN2 41 F3
Holden Gv DAV NN11 50 D2
The Hollies NHTNE/MOU NN3 24 B2
RSHD/HF NN10 19 F4
WBORO NN8 15 G4
Hollingside Dr
NHTNN/BOU NN2 41 G4
Hollington Rd IR/RAU/FIN NN9 11 F2
Hollow Bank NHTNE/MOU NN3 42 C1
Hollowell Cl RSHD/HF NN10 33 H4
Holly Lodge Dr
NHTNN/BOU NN2 41 E2
Holly Rd NHTN NN1 55 H2
RSHD/HF NN10 32 C1
Holly Wk IR/RAU/FIN NN9 7 F2
Holman Cl NHTNE/MOU NN3 42 D5
Holm Cl RNHPTN NN7 62 C5
Holme Cl IR/RAU/FIN NN9 6 A5
Holmecross Rd
NHTNE/MOU NN3 43 E2
Holmes Av IR/RAU/FIN NN9 11 F3
Holmfield Dr IR/RAU/FIN NN9 11 G2
Holmfield Wy
NHTNE/MOU NN3 56 C2
Holmleigh Cl NHTNW NN5 53 G3
Holmwood Cl NHTNW NN5 53 E1
Holyoake Rd
BOZ/IR/WOL NN29 48 D3
Holyrood Rd NHTNW NN5 54 B3
Home Acre RNHPTN NN7 71 H2
Home Cl IR/RAU/FIN NN9 18 C1
RNHPTN NN7 79 F4
Home Farm Cl
NHTNE/MOU NN3 57 H2
Home Farm La
BRIX/LBKBY NN6 13 E5
Homefield DAV NN11 51 E4
Homestead Cl
NHTNE/MOU NN3 24 D3
Homestead Dr RNHPTN NN7 65 G5
Homestead Ri NHTNS NN4 76 C2
Homestead Wy
NHTNN/BOU NN2 55 G1
Honey Holme BRIX/LBKBY NN6 4 C5
Honeystones NHTNE/MOU NN3 24 C3
Honeysuckle Wy
NHTNE/MOU NN3 56 C4
Hood Rd DAV NN11 51 G2
Hood St NHTN NN1 55 G3
Hookhams Pth
BOZ/IR/WOL NN29 49 E3
Hopes Pl NHTNN/BOU NN2 40 D4
Hope St BOZ/IR/WOL NN29 61 F3
Hopmeadow Ct
NHTNE/MOU NN3 43 H3
Hopping Hill Gdns NHTNW NN5 53 H1
Hopton Cl DAV NN11 35 E3
Hornbeam Cl WBORO NN8 15 G4
Hornbeam Ct
NHTNE/MOU NN3 42 D4
Hornby Rd BRIX/LBKBY NN6 46 A2
Horsemarket NHTN NN1 2 C4
Horsemoor Sq
NHTNE/MOU NN3 44 A5
Horseshoe Cl BRIX/LBKBY NN6 5 E4
Horse Well Ct
NHTNE/MOU NN3 24 C5
Horsley Rd NHTNN/BOU NN2 54 D1
Horton Rd RNHPTN NN7 72 B4
Houghton Hl NHTNS NN4 69 H4
Hove Rd RSHD/HF NN10 33 G2
Howard Biley Gdns
NHTNE/MOU NN3 42 C4
Howard Cl DAV NN11 51 F3
Howard La NHTNN/BOU NN2 23 E5
Howard Rd BOZ/IR/WOL NN29 48 D3
Howards Wy
NHTNE/MOU NN3 42 B2
Howe Crs DAV NN11 51 G3
Hoylake WBORO NN8 15 E2
Hoylake Dr NHTNN/BOU NN2 41 H4
Hudson Cl DAV NN11 35 E4
Hudson Dr NHTNS NN4 67 H4
Hulme Wy WBORO NN8 15 G2
Humber Cl DAV NN11 34 B5
NHTNW NN5 40 A5
Humber Gdns WBORO NN8 15 E3
Humfrey La NHTNN/BOU NN2 23 E4
Hunsbarrow Rd NHTNS NN4 68 A1
Hunsbury Cl NHTNS NN4 68 A4
Hunsbury Gn NHTNS NN4 67 H3
Hunsbury Hill Av NHTNS NN4 68 A2
Hunsbury Hill Rd NHTNS NN4 68 A3
Hunslet La NHTNS NN4 68 A4
Hunt Cl BRIX/LBKBY NN6 4 D4
WBORO NN8 15 H1
Hunters Cl NHTNN/BOU NN2 41 F1
Hunters' Wy BRIX/LBKBY NN6 4 D4
Huntsham Cl NHTNE/MOU NN3 56 D3
Huntsmead NHTNE/MOU NN3 44 B3
Hussar Cl DAV NN11 50 D3
Huxley Cl WBORO NN8 14 B5
Huxloe Ri NHTNE/MOU NN3 43 E1
Hyacinth Wy RSHD/HF NN10 33 F5
Hyde Cl RNHPTN NN7 80 C4
Hyde Dr IR/RAU/FIN NN9 8 A1
Hyde Rd RNHPTN NN7 80 C4

I

Ibstock Cl NHTNE/MOU NN3 43 G1
Icknield Dr NHTNS NN4 68 A4
Ickworth Cl DAV NN11 34 D2
Ilex Cl NHTNS NN4 69 H4
Ilmor Av BRIX/LBKBY NN6 5 F2
Indmere Cl NHTNS NN4 67 G4
Inglewood Ct
NHTNE/MOU NN3 58 A1
Inlands Cl DAV NN11 51 F3
Inlands Ri DAV NN11 51 F3
The Inlands DAV NN11 51 F3
Insignia Cl NHTNS NN4 76 C1
Irchester Rd
BOZ/IR/WOL NN29 49 F2
RSHD/HF NN10 32 C2
Iron Pikes BRIX/LBKBY NN6 5 E5
Ironstone La NHTNS NN4 68 A2
Ironstone Wy BRIX/LBKBY NN6 5 E3
Irthlingborough Rd
IR/RAU/FIN NN9 8 A2
WBORO NN8 30 B1
Isham Cl NHTNN/BOU NN2 41 F2
Ivy La IR/RAU/FIN NN9 7 H2
Ivy Rd NHTN NN1 55 H2
Ixworth Cl NHTNE/MOU NN3 43 F2

J

Jackdaw Cl NHTNE/MOU NN3 58 A2
Jack English Cl NHTNW NN5 53 F3
Jacklin Ct WBORO NN8 15 E2
Jack Parnell Cl NHTNW NN5 53 F3
Jackson Cl NHTNN/BOU NN2 41 G1
Jacksons La WBORO NN8 15 H5
Jacorrin Cl NHTNN/BOU NN2 41 G1
James Lewis Ct
NHTNE/MOU NN3 42 C5
James Rd WBORO NN8 30 A3
James St BOZ/IR/WOL NN29 31 H5
James Watt Cl DAV NN11 34 B5
Jardine Cl NHTNE/MOU NN3 56 D1
Jarretts Yd NHTNS NN4 76 C2
Jasmine Gdns RSHD/HF NN10 33 F5
Jasmine Rd NHTNE/MOU NN3 44 A2
Javelin Cl NHTNW NN5 53 G2
Jellicoe Cl DAV NN11 51 G3
Jenner Crs NHTNN/BOU NN2 40 D2
Jennings Cl DAV NN11 51 F3
RSHD/HF NN10 19 F4
Jersey Cl WBORO NN8 16 B3
Jersey Ct NHTNE/MOU NN3 57 F1
Jervis Cl DAV NN11 51 G3
Jeyes Cl NHTNE/MOU NN3 24 B3
Joan Pyel Cl IR/RAU/FIN NN9 18 C1
John Clark Wy RSHD/HF NN10 33 F1
John Eagle Cl IR/RAU/FIN NN9 10 B4
John Gray Rd
BOZ/IR/WOL NN29 47 F1
John Lea Wy WBORO NN8 30 A3
John Pyel Rd IR/RAU/FIN NN9 9 E5
Johnson Av WBORO NN8 30 A3
Johnson Cl DAV NN11 50 D1
Johnson Ct NHTNS NN4 2 E6
Johns Rd RNHPTN NN7 65 G4
John St RSHD/HF NN10 33 F2
The John White Cl
RSHD/HF NN10 19 G3
Joshua Sq NHTNS NN4 68 B3
Jubilee Cl NHTNS NN4 68 B2
Jubilee Crs WBORO NN8 29 H2
Jubilee Gdns RSHD/HF NN10 33 G4
Jubilee Rd DAV NN11 50 D2
Jubilee St IR/RAU/FIN NN9 9 E4
Julian Wy NHTNN/BOU NN2 40 C4
Junction Rd NHTNN/BOU NN2 55 G1
Juniper Ct NHTNE/MOU NN3 44 B4
Juniper Thorn BRIX/LBKBY NN6 5 E5

K

Kangaroo Spinney
WBORO NN8 30 D1
Kealdale Rd NHTNE/MOU NN3 42 A3
Keats Cl BRIX/LBKBY NN6 46 B4
NHTNS NN4 71 F4
Keats Rd DAV NN11 50 D1
WBORO NN8 15 F5
Keats Wy RSHD/HF NN10 32 C2
Keble Cl DAV NN11 50 D4
Kedleston Cl NHTNS NN4 69 E5
Keepers Cl NHTNS NN4 76 D5
Kelburn Cl NHTNS NN4 75 H1
Kelmscott Cl NHTNE/MOU NN3 43 G2
Kelsall Cl NHTNW NN5 53 F2
Kendal Cl NHTNE/MOU NN3 42 D3
RSHD/HF NN10 33 G3
WBORO NN8 15 E3
Kenilworth Cl DAV NN11 50 D3
NHTNW NN5 53 F2
RSHD/HF NN10 33 G3
Kenmuir Av NHTNN/BOU NN2 41 H5
Kenmuir Crs NHTNN/BOU NN2 41 H5
Kenmuir Gdns
NHTNN/BOU NN2 41 H5
Kenmuir Rd IR/RAU/FIN NN9 7 H2
Kennedy Cl DAV NN11 51 G3
Kennel Ter BRIX/LBKBY NN6 4 D4
Kennet Cl WBORO NN8 14 D3
Kennet Gn NHTNW NN5
Kensington Cl RSHD/HF NN
Kent Cl NHTNW NN5
Kentford Cl NHTNS NN4
Kent Rd NHTNW NN5
RSHD/HF NN10
WBORO NN8
Kentstone Cl NHTNN/BOU N
Kerrfield Est NHTNW NN5
Keston Wy IR/RAU/FIN NN9
Kestrel Cl NHTNE/MOU NN3
Kestrel La WBORO NN8
Keswick Dr NHTNE/MOU NN
RSHD/HF NN10
Kettering Gdns NHTN NN1
Kettering Rd IR/RAU/FIN NN
NHTNE/MOU NN3
NHTNE/MOU NN3
Kettering Rd North
NHTNE/MOU NN3
Keyham Ct NHTNE/MOU NN
Keys Cl DAV NN11
Keystone NHTNS NN4
Kilborn Cl WBORO NN8
Kilborn Rd WBORO NN8
Kilburn Pl RSHD/HF NN10
Kilby Cl WBORO NN8
Kiln La DAV NN11
Kilnway WBORO NN8
Kilvey Rd NHTNS NN4
Kimble Cl NHTNS NN4
Kimbolton Rd RSHD/HF NN1
King Edward Rd NHTN NN1
Kingfisher Cl NHTNS NN4
Kingfisher Ct BRIX/LBKBY N
Kingmaker Wy NHTNS NN4
King Richard Ct NHTNS NN4
Kings Av RSHD/HF NN10
Kings Cl NHTNS NN4
Kingscroft Ct
NHTNE/MOU NN3
Kingsfield Cl NHTNW NN5
Kingsfield Wy NHTNW NN5
Kings Gn DAV NN11
Kingsland Av NHTNN/BOU N
Kingsland Cl NHTNN/BOU N
Kingsland Gdns
NHTNN/BOU NN2
King's La RNHPTN NN7
Kingsley Av DAV NN11
Kingsley Gdns
NHTNN/BOU NN2
Kingsley Rd NHTNN/BOU NN
Kingsmead NHTNN/BOU NN2
Kings Meadow La
RSHD/HF NN10
Kingsmead Pk RSHD/HF NN1
Kingsmith Dr IR/RAU/FIN NN
Kings Pk RNHPTN NN7
Kings Park Rd
NHTNE/MOU NN3
Kings Pl RSHD/HF NN10
Kings Rd RSHD/HF NN10
Kings St WBORO NN8
Kingsthorpe Gv
NHTNN/BOU NN2
Kingsthorpe Rd
NHTNN/BOU NN2
Kingston Cl DAV NN11
King St BRIX/LBKBY NN6
NHTN NN1
Kingsway NHTNN/BOU NN2
WBORO NN8
Kingswell Rd NHTNN/BOU N
Kingswell St NHTN NN1
Kinross Cl NHTNE/MOU NN3
Kirby Cl NHTNS NN4
Kirton Cl NHTNE/MOU NN3
Kirton End NHTNE/MOU NN3
Kislingbury Rd RNHPTN NN7
Kitchener Cl DAV NN11
Kites Cl NHTNS NN4
Knaphill Crs NHTNS NN4
Knightlands Rd
IR/RAU/FIN NN9
Knightley Rd NHTNN/BOU N
Knighton Cl NHTNW NN5
Knightons Wy
BRIX/LBKBY NN6
Knightscliffe Wy NHTNW NN5
Knights Cl BOZ/IR/WOL NN29
BRIX/LBKBY NN6
Knights Ct NHTNE/MOU NN3
WBORO NN8
Knight's La NHTNN/BOU NN2
The Knoll BRIX/LBKBY NN6
RNHPTN NN7
Knowle Cl NHTNE/MOU NN3
Knowles Cl RSHD/HF NN10
Knowle Wy DAV NN11
Knox Rd WBORO NN8
Kyoto Cl NHTNE/MOU NN3

L

Laburnham Cl WBORO NN8
Laburnum Crs
NHTNE/MOU NN3
Lacemakers Ct RSHD/HF NN1
Ladybridge Dr NHTNS NN4
Lady Cft DAV NN11
Ladyfield RNHPTN NN7
Lady Hollows Dr NHTNS NN4
Ladymead Cl NHTNS NN4
Lady's La BRIX/LBKBY NN6
NHTN NN1
Lady Winefride's Wk
NHTNE/MOU NN3
Lake Crs DAV NN11
Lakeside IR/RAU/FIN NN9
NHTNE/MOU NN3
NHTNS NN4
Lakeside Dr NHTNE/MOU NN3
The Lakes NHTNS NN4
Lake Wk NHTNS NN4
Lambrook Dr NHTNS NN4
Lamport Dr DAV NN11